D1474146

Freedom Road

Adult Education of African Americans

EDITED BY
ELIZABETH A. PETERSON

KRIEGER PUBLISHING COMPANY
MALABAR, FLORIDA
2002

Original Edition 1996
Revised Edition 2002

Printed and Published by
KRIEGER PUBLISHING COMPANY
KRIEGER DRIVE
MALABAR, FLORIDA 32950

Copyright © 1996, 2002 by Krieger Publishing Company

Library of Congress Cataloging-in-Publication Data

Freedom road : adult education of African Americans / edited by Elizabeth A. Peterson.—Rev. ed.
    p. cm.
  Includes bibliographical references and index.
  ISBN 1-57524-208-7 (alk. paper)
    1. African Americans—Education (Continuing education). 2. Adult education—United States. I. Peterson, Elizabeth A., 1956-

  LC2780.8 .F74 2002
  374'.00896'073—dc21

                       2001038862

10   9   8   7   6   5   4   3   2

CONTENTS

ACKNOWLEDGMENTS

All works of this kind are the result of the efforts of many people. I would like to mention a few of the people who made this book possible. First of all thanks to Dr. Phyllis Cunningham. Phyllis has always supported the notion that African Americans should have a role of leadership in the adult education field. She believed along with many others that African American contributions have been too long neglected and has played an instrumental role in seeing that African American scholars have a chance to be heard. I would also like to thank Dr. Burton Sisco, who has shown so much patience. He and other members of the Publications Standing Service Unit of the American Association of Adult and Continuing Education have supported this project and seen it through to its completion. I would like to thank Drs. Harold Stubblefield, Anthony Mitchell, and Edwin Hamilton, who reviewed the manuscript for this book not once, but twice. All three offered many suggestions which really did strengthen the book, but even more important was their support. Never did they offer criticism without saying at the same time that this was a very important work. Thanks to my sister, Rebecca Peterson, for her fine editing skills, and also to Cindy Grugan, my secretary, for all her help in typing and formatting the final draft. Finally I would like to thank all of the wonderful African American students and scholars that I have met in the past year. It is the inspiration and encouragement that I have received from all of you that makes this work possible.

Contributors

Scipio A.J. Colin, III is an Associate Professor of Adult and Continuing Education at National Louis University in Chicago, Illinois. Dr. Colin received a B.A. degree from Roosevelt University and an M.A. in Urban Studies from Northeastern Illinois University. After postgraduate studies at the University of Chicago, Dr. Colin earned an Ed.D. in Adult and Continuing Education from Northern Illinois University.

Opal V. Easter is the Director of Continuing Education and Ministerial Formation for the Catholic Theological Union, the largest Catholic graduate school of Theology and Ministry in the U.S. She spent 18 years in continuing education with the City Colleges of Chicago before retiring to take the position at CTU. She received her B.S. degree from DePaul University in Chicago, and earned both her M.S. degree and Ed.D. in Adult and Continuing Education from Northern Illinois University.

Talmadge C. Guy is an Associate Professor of Adult Education at the University of Georgia in Athens, Georgia. He received a B.A. degree from Fisk University in Nashville, Tennessee, and a M.A. from Northwestern University before earning an Ed.D. in Adult and Continuing Education from Northern Illinois University.

LaVerne Gyant is the Director of the Center for Black Studies and an Associate Professor of Counseling, Adult, and Health Education at Northern Illinois University. Dr. Gyant received a B.S. degree from Cheyney State University of Pennsylvania and then earned an M.S. degree in Home Economics and an Ed.D. in Adult Education from the Pennsylvania State University.

Elizabeth A. Peterson is an Associate Professor and Coordinator of Community Education Programs at the Institute on Family and Neighborhood Life at Clemson University in South Carolina. Dr. Peterson received a B.S. degree in Multicultural Education and an M.S. degree in Adult Education from Indiana University in Bloomington, Indiana. She completed an Ed.D. in Adult and Continuing Education at Northern Illinois University.

Edward Potts is a Research Associate at the Institute on Family and Neighborhood Life at Clemson University in South Carolina. Mr. Potts received a B.A. degree from Roosevelt University in Chicago. He later earned a M.A. in Social Work from the University of Illinois at Chicago and a Master of Management from Northwestern University.

Andrew Smallwood is an Assistant Professor in the Black Studies Department at the University of Nebraska at Omaha. Dr. Smallwood received his Bachelor's and Master's degrees from the Pennsylvania State University and an Ed.D. in Adult and Continuing Education from Northern Illinois University.

FOREWORD

A series of African American adult education research symposia was developed by Northern Illinois University black graduate students in Chicago starting in 1991, culminating in a national conference on the "African American Research Agenda" held prior to the 1993 Adult Education Research Conference at Penn State University. Black graduate students meeting at the National Conference, where 28 papers were presented by African American researchers, spoke about making history with this breakthrough conference where adult educators were meeting nationally to focus on the African American experience and the field of adult education.

Tony Fitchue (Teacher's College) took the group by surprise when he reported on his research on Alain Locke. This group learned for the first time that Alain Locke had convened four national conferences on "Adult Education and the Negro." The official sponsors of these conferences were the Associates in Negro Folk Education, Hampton Institute, and the American Association for Adult Education (AAAE), forerunner of the American Association of Adult Continuing Education (AAACE). The four conferences were funded by the Carnegie Corporation and held at Hampton Institute (1938), Tuskegee College (1940), Howard University (1941), and Atlanta University (1942). Two observations are noteworthy. First, it was fifty years later that the fifth conference occurred, and this time it was not the professional association or a foundation that caused it to happen—it came up from the field through black graduate students. Second, it is interesting to note that the AAAE was strongly involved in these four conferences, having just completed two major "Negro experiments," the Harlem and Atlanta projects (1931–34). Ambrose Caliver had just published a major report supported by the U.S. Office of Education on the *Vocational Education and Guidance of Negroes* which made clear the underrepresentation of African Americans in vocational adult education. Alain Locke had solicited funds and authors for a series of "pamphlets on negro life and culture" which became the Bronze Booklets. Both of these African American adult educators served as presidents of the AAAE. Under their leadership the association confronted racism in society with efforts including two major projects on Negro adult education, the Bronze Booklets series, and four national conferences to address the problem. Our professional association was interacting with the Historic Black Colleges and leaders of the Harlem Renaissance. Two questions came to mind as I listened to these young black scholars at Penn State: 1) Why have we lost this history of antiracist activity of adult educator professionals when we were able to preserve the history of the Junto, the Chautauqua, the Lyceums, and the Mechanics Institutes? and 2) Why does the Association today appear to avoid such major social issues as racism facing our society?

It seems to me that publishing this book is a statement by the AAACE Executive Board and its publications unit that we need to change. Under the leadership of President William S. Griffith, the Publications Standing Service Unit of AAACE commissioned *Freedom Road: Adult Education of African Americans.* At the same time a committee on "inclusivity" was commissioned by Griffith to study any internal barriers to full participation within the association. In fact one could see as early as 1990 at the AAACE conference in Salt Lake City that the planners wanted to involve the members in a debate around *issues* facing the field. Staging "On Trial: The Education of Adults," the judges and jury found the Association guilty of losing its "commitment to the field's historic sense of social action."

The AAACE is pleased to present *Freedom Road: Adult Education of African Americans,* where editor Elizabeth A. Peterson and her African American colleagues have provided us with a beginning history of African Americans' contributions and participation in adult education. The chapters by Talmadge C. Guy, Scipio A.J. Colin, III, Edward Potts, and LaVerne Gyant bring us face to face with the black intellectuals who brought energy and ideas to adult education. Foremost was Alain Locke, a leading intellectual of the Harlem Renaissance who spent years in active leadership in the AAAE. W.E.B. Du Bois and Booker T. Washington, well known as protagonists of philosophy of education,

Kelly Miller who saw learning from a cultural context, Marcus Garvey who understood the politics of adult education, all made a conceptual contribution to adult education. Two chapters celebrate the role of African American women in adult education, and Elizabeth A. Peterson and Opal V. Easter remind us that education of adults takes place, not only as part of a social movement as exemplified by Septima Clark and the 1960s Civil Rights Movement, but also through schools such as the experimental Institute for Colored Youth organized by Fanny Jackson Coppin, or integrated country schools championed by Mary Ann Shadd Cary, or the literacy programs for newly freed slaves as promoted by abolitionist Charlotte Forten Grimke.

This book is written for two purposes: First, it will begin to fill the "structured silences" in graduate curriculums on African American history. Within this book are also many of the issues that face us today: Afrocentrism, cultural pluralism, biculturalism, cultural contexts of learning, education for liberation (transformation), gender issues which intersect racism, tracking, learning for earning, and on and on. Second, the thousands of teachers of adults, many who are African American, need to revisit their commitment to diversity by deciding whose voices will be heard in our educational settings and to examine the scripts and the "underneath" of the stories (theories, rationales) we extol. If we really celebrate diversity, let us celebrate the African American traditions, heros, and symbols by including such books as *Freedom Road* in our teaching and adult education practice.

Phyllis M. Cunningham
Chair, AAACE Publications Standing Service
Unit (1990–91)
and Professor of Adult Education,
Northern Illinois University

INTRODUCTION
ELIZABETH A. PETERSON

On January 1, 1863, the Emancipation Proclamation declared that
"all persons held as slaves within any State. . . shall be then,
thenceforth, and forever free." These words gave black men and
women the legal right to freedom, but in reality Emancipation was just
the beginning of the long, often perilous journey toward freedom.
What was changed overnight on paper would take many years to
change in the hearts and minds of people.

During the years immediately following the Civil War, newly
freed African Americans struggled to acquire the education and
skills that would enable them to prosper as free men and women. It
is evident that black people felt that education was the way to gain
equality. Using every avenue available to them, they set out to educate
themselves. Booker T. Washington in later years was to write:

> This experience of a whole race beginning to go to school for the
> first time presents one of the most interesting studies that has ever
> occurred in connection with the development of any race. Few
> people who were not right in the midst of the scenes can form
> any exact idea of the intense desire which the people of my race
> showed for an education. As I have stated, it was a whole race try-
> ing to go to school. Few were too young, and none too old, to
> make the attempt to learn. As fast as any kind of teachers could
> be secured, not only were day-schools filled, but night-schools
> as well. . . Day-school, night-school, Sunday-school, were al-
> ways crowded, and often many had to be turned away for want of
> room.[1]

It is clear from this passage that African Americans truly believed
that education was the road to freedom. It is interesting to note that
for the former slaves little distinction was made between children
and adults in the classroom. All needed to learn. Adult education
played as vital a role as child education in the struggle for freedom.

Black people had long been denied access to schools, books, and
teachers by their white masters who believed that education would

"spoil" the slaves for their lives of labor by making them dissatisfied with their positions. After the Civil War these same people believed that education for the "Negro" was a dangerous thing. Because of this fear African Americans who had been threatened and victimized as slaves found themselves often still threatened and victimized as free men and women. Their schools were often the targets of vandalism and violence. Yet the struggle has continued.

The story of how the African American people have struggled to educate themselves—from slavery to freedom—is one that needs to be told. It is also important that readers understand the sometimes opposing values and beliefs held by African American leaders and educators. While all believed that freedom was the ultimate goal, they often differed vehemently on what freedom was and how it should be achieved. These opposing beliefs have been the foundation for the struggle as we know it today. The educational programs and practices of African Americans reflect these beliefs.

The purpose of this book is twofold. First it will give the reader insight into how some African American leaders saw the connection between education and the eventual freedom or uplift of the African American people. By doing this it will bring to light some of the beliefs about education and freedom which have at times caused friction among African American leaders and educators. It has often mistakenly believed that the black community speaks with one voice. As in all communities the black community is made up of people of diverse backgrounds, values, and philosophical orientations. It is also our hope that this book will introduce readers to individuals who have made a tremendous contribution to African American adult education. Some of the names which appear in this volume may be familiar while others are, perhaps, more obscure. However, all of these individuals shared the dream of African American uplift and freedom and committed their lives to making this dream a reality.

Chapter 1 is appropriately subtitled, "Three African American Women Who Made a Difference." It traces the lives and accomplishments of three black female teachers: Fanny Jackson Coppin, Mary Ann Shadd Cary, and Charlotte Forten Grimke. These women all devoted their lives to black freedom, yet one can easily see how each had a different perspective. Chapter 2 revisits the rivalry between two well-known black leaders, Booker T. Washington and W. E. B. Du Bois. Although many may be familiar with the dispute between the two that followed Booker T. Washington's now infamous "Atlanta Compromise," it might not be as evident how each man's very different background molded his life.

They could not see eye to eye because their life experiences had give them different vision.

At the same time that Washington and Du Bois were entangled in bitter debate, Marcus Garvey was promoting a still different plan for freedom. In Chapter 3 Marcus Garvey's tremendous effort is revealed. In many ways Garvey was overshadowed by Washington and Du Bois, but his leadership and important accomplishments should not be ignored. His primary project, the Universal Negro Improvement Association-African Communities League (UNIA-ACL), was perhaps one of the most ambitious and comprehensive programs for African American empowerment ever initiated.

Chapter 4 is titled "Alain Leroy Locke: More that an Adult Educator." Many are familiar with Alain Locke as a scholar and know of his primary role during the Harlem Renaissance, but his role as an adult educator is less well known. The Harlem Renaissance has often been considered the "golden age of African American culture and artistic acceptance. Harlem served as a mecca for the "brightest and best" of black minds and the most talented black artists. No one contributed more to the spirit of the Harlem Renaissance than Alain Locke. Himself a brilliant scholar, he attracted others of equal brilliance. He had a knack for identifying fine minds and helping them to develop. He recognized before many others the importance of adult education for African Americans and was on the cutting edge as adult education emerges as a newly developing professional field.

In Chapter 5 the Harlem Renaissance is again the focus, but this time the influence of white philanthropy during the Harlem Renaissance is discussed, in particular that of the Carnegie Corporation, which sponsored two experimental projects during this time. The Harlem and Atlanta Experiments in Adult Education were pilot projects initiated to "test" adult education in an African American context and to determine to some extent what kind of adult education was most appropriate for blacks. Alain Locke emerges once again as the central figure in this chapter.

The "Freedom Road" becomes rougher and rockier as Chapter 6 takes the reader into the turbulent 1960's and the Civil Rights Movement. One of he most important educational programs during this time was the voter registration drive, and the force behind this drive was Septima Poinsette Clark. This chapter takes a look at this dedicated woman and the literacy program that she designed.

In this updated edition of *Freedom Road* a new chapter has been added that explores the role that Malcolm X, a minister in the Nation of Islam and Civil Rights activist, played as an adult educator.

Malcolm X engaged the nation and the black community in an intellectual public discourse at a critical point in African American history. He raised issues and set forth an agenda for African American empowerment. His life and his words still inspire.

The book concludes with a brief look at where we are today. At the dawn of the twenty-first century, is the journey on the Freedom Road complete or do we just find ourselves on a new path? After the Civil Rights Movement many people thought that the struggle and strife of that period had settled most of the problems of inequality. During the final decades of the twentieth century more African Americans prospered than ever before. African Americans hold prominent positions and are represented in every arena. Yet as we take a closer look we find that more and more African Americans have been left behind in situations of poverty and despair. In the inner city black youths are abandoning the schools which they feel have abandoned them. For young people who lack skills there are few opportunities and gangs offer more comfort and security for some than the family, the church, or the schools.

Even for those who have prospered there are many issues that have not been resolved. Due to racial profiling and stereotyping African American men and women are often still at a disadvantage, even if they come from middle class homes. Affirmative Action has come under fire with claims that the policy has created circumstances of reverse discrimination. Once again African Americans leaders are debating what needs to be done to guarantee the rights of all. Some leaders say that self-discipline and hard work alone will lift poor blacks from poverty, the time of Affirmative Action has passed. Others believe that racial prejudice and discrimination still play a major role in our social and economic systems today and that the laws and policies like Affirmative Action provide a safeguard against discrimination. Still others believe that the only way the black community will survive and thrive is through separation and self-determination. No matter what direction we take, it is clear that education, adult education, will always play a vital role in the growth and development of the African American community. In the twenty-first century we begin a new journey on the Freedom Road.

NOTES

1. Booker T. Washington, *Up From Slavery* (New York: Avon Books, 1965). pp. 44-45.

CHAPTER 1

FANNY COPPIN, MARY SHADD CARY, AND CHARLOTTE GRIMKE: THREE AFRICAN AMERICAN WOMEN WHO MADE A DIFFERENCE

ELIZABETH A. PETERSON

> "It was in me to get an education and to teach my people. This idea was deep in my soul. Where it came from I cannot tell. . . . It must have been born in me."[1]

These words were written by Fanny Jackson Coppin, a black woman who devoted her life to the education of her people. Fanny Coppin's accomplishments as an educator, along with those of other black female educators, have gone virtually unnoticed. Yet black women have been in many ways the backbone of their community, at the heart of every struggle, and nowhere have their contributions been more pronounced than in education.

Although black women have been prominent in most facets of American life, their role in the education of their race has been their most salient contribution. While twentieth-century [black female educators are better known, the contributors of their nineteenth-century] sisters have been overshadowed as a consequence of several factors. These are namely, the emphasis placed in history upon the role of the Northern white female school teacher, benevolent and philanthropic organizations, and Booker T. Washington's industrial philosophy of the late nineteenth century.[2]

Even more obscure is the role that African American women have played in adult education. The Civil War and Reconstruction spurred a great deal of educational activity and in fact "the struggle of education for the freedman was, by definition adult education."[3] Much of this activity was initiated by white benevolent and missionary societies. The American Missionary Association alone supported more than five thousand teachers in the South between 1861 and 1876.[4] They were by far the largest of the missionary societies. Other associations involved in the education of freed slaves were the Friends Associations of Philadelphia and New York, the Pennsylvania Freedman's Relief Association, New England Freedmen's Aid Society and the Freedmen's Aid Society of the Methodist Episcopal Church. There was a general belief among abolitionists, missionaries, and black leaders that education, which had been long denied, was critical if African American people were to know any true freedom. While it cannot be denied that white philanthropy and support of education was instrumental and that the educational programs were probably the most important and long-lasting achievement of the aid societies, the African American's commitment to self-help must not be ignored.

> The black American journey is one of making a way out of no way because we often had no one, save God, to lend us a hand. For most of our American sojourn government has been opponent and victimizer rather than ally. Slavery and legally sanctioned segregation left to us the major burden of seeking our own freedom.[5]

Fanny Jackson Coppin, Mary Ann Shadd Cary, and Charlotte Forten all made significant contributions not only as educators, but also as advocates, lecturers, and leaders in a day when women were not encouraged to speak. These three women dedicated their lives to uplifting their race. It is interesting to note that each of these women entered the struggle for freedom at a very young age. They delayed marriage and personal pursuits, which was uncommon for that day (All three women were in their late thirties or early forties before they married. Charlotte Forten gave birth to her first child at age forty-three. Fanny Jackson and Mary Ann Shadd both lived for extended periods away from their husbands to pursue their own careers). These women were primarily teachers who saw education as the instrument for creating a race of proud people, a race of people who were inferior to no other. Each woman had a philosophy as different as her background and yet they each worked to one end, complete freedom for African American people.

FANNY JACKSON COPPIN
1837–1913

Early Years

Fanny Jackson was born a slave in Washington, D.C. in 1837. Jackson's grandfather had long before bought his freedom and later bought four of his six children. He did not buy Fanny's mother due to the "circumstances of her (Fanny's) birth."[6] Fanny was purchased, however, during childhood by her Aunt Sarah and moved to New Bedford, Massachusetts to live with another aunt. Fanny began school in New Bedford, attending classes whenever she was not working. At the age of fourteen Fanny moved to Newport, Rhode Island to live with yet another aunt with the hopes of getting an even better education. While in Newport she obtained a position in the home of George H. Calvert and Elizabeth Stuart Calvert. The Calvert's were aristocratic people who took a liking to the young girl and therefore did not object to her pursuit of education. For a while she took private lessons and when these ended she attended the "colored" public school. She even set aside money from her wages to take private piano lessons at her aunt's home. It is interesting that while her benefactor, Mrs. Calvert, was very fond of Fanny, Fanny kept her piano lessons a secret for fear that her employer would not approve.

Fanny realized at this young age that her mission was "to teach her people" and in a short time she had prepared herself to take the examination for the Rhode Island State Normal School located in Bristol, Rhode Island. She excelled as a student and completed the normal course in 1860. That same year she enrolled in Oberlin College in Ohio. Oberlin College was unique. Founded in 1834, the college admitted women from the very beginning, but it is also known because it is recognized as being the first school which also admitted blacks.

At Oberlin, Fanny studied Latin, Greek, and mathematics. She also took private lessons in French, which was not part of the curriculum. While at Oberlin, Fanny first realized her dream of becoming a teacher. She began a small evening school to teach freedmen who migrated to Oberlin. As a result of this class, Fanny's exceptional teaching abilities were recognized by college officials and she was chosen to be the first black student teacher in the Preparatory Department of Oberlin College.[7] This was no small honor in these days. In a time when many whites were trying to prove the inferiority of the Negro race, Fanny's achievements created quite a stir. By the time she left Oberlin in 1865, she had gained world recognition as an outstanding educator. This was an honor that Fanny took very seriously. She believed that she had an obligation to her people. She wrote,

> I never rose to recite in my classes at Oberlin but I felt that I had the honor of the whole African race upon my shoulders. I felt that, should I fail, it would be ascribed to the fact that I was colored.[8]

The Institute for Colored Youth

Fanny Jackson graduated from Oberlin College in 1865 and went to Philadelphia to teach at the Institute for Colored Youth (ICY) in Philadelphia. The school which was founded and financed by the Society of Friends was one of the first institutions of higher learning for African Americans. In 1865 the school was in the process of becoming a full-fledged classical high school and normal school.[9] The Institute had requested the year before that Oberlin send them a colored woman who could teach Latin, Greek, and high mathematics. Officials at Oberlin wrote back that they had such a woman, but the Institute would have to wait a year for her.[10] So Fanny Jackson arrived in Philadelphia in 1865 to an eagerly awaiting black community.[11]

Fanny Jackson was promoted to principal of ICY in 1869. Ebenezer Bassett, then principal of the Institute, was appointed U.S. Minister to Haiti. When Fanny Jackson was promoted to his position by the Quaker managers of the school, she became the first black female to head an institute of higher learning. Under her leadership the school quickly changed and expanded its normal school program. Following the Civil War there was an increased demand for black teachers who could teach the basics—reading, writing, and mathematics. Fanny believed that the time spent in teaching Latin and Greek could be better spent in a normal program. The normal school program became so popular and the students so sought after that many were able to attain employment before they completed their studies.

Fanny Jackson's philosophy was simple. She believed that it was her role to unlock whatever potential was within each one of her students. The Institute's curriculum had been designed primarily to showcase black intellectual capability, yet she was concerned that there was a lack of training for blacks in the skilled trades. Fanny Jackson was a prudent woman. She knew that a classical education was not good enough to prepare the masses of black men and women for a changing job market.[12] She did not believe that a person should be trained as a lawyer when he would make a better mechanic nor should a person who had the mind to be an engineer be wasted in doing manual activities.

Fanny Jackson believed that African Americans would achieve an elevated status only if they received an education that combined scholarly preparation with practical skills and applications that would make them employable. In 1876 in a letter to Frederick Douglass she wrote of her continued desire to see African American people esteemed and respected:

I feel sometimes like a person to whom in childhood was entrusted some sacred flame: it has burned more dimly sometimes than at others, but it always has and always will, burn steadily and persistently for it will never go out but with my life. I need not tell you, Mr. Douglass, that this is the desire to see my race lifted out of the mire of ignorance, weakness and degradation: no longer to sit in obscure corners and devour the scraps of knowledge which his superiors fling him. I want to see him crowned with strength and dignity; adorned with the enduring grace of intellectual attainments, and a lover of manly deeds and downright honesty.[13]

Nowhere were her desires more evident than in her struggle to begin industrial training at the Institute for Colored Youth. She wrote,

Before all the literary societies and churches where they would hear me; in Philadelphia and the suburban towns; in New York, Washington and everywhere, when invited to speak, I made that (industrial education) one subject my theme. To equip an industrial plant is an expensive thing, and knowing that much money would be needed, I made it a rule to take up a collection wheresoever I spoke. But I did not urge anyone to give more than a dollar, for the reason I wanted the masses to have an opportunity to contribute their small offerings, before going to those who were able to give larger sums.[14]

and later,

At a meeting of some of the public school directors and heads of some of the educational institutions, I was asked to tell what was being done in Philadelphia for the industrial education of the colored youth. It may well be understood I had a tale to tell. And I told them the only places in the city where a colored boy could learn a trade was in the House of Refuge or the Penitentiary, and the sooner he became incorrigible and got into the Refuge, or committed a crime and got into the Penitentiary, the more promising it would be for his industrial training.[15]

The first industrial courses established at the school included bricklaying, plastering, carpentry, shoe making, printing, and tailoring for the men and dressmaking, millinery, typewriting, and stenography for the women. Courses in cooking were offered for both sexes.

Through continued speeches and fundraising efforts Fanny Jackson was able to not only raise money for the Institute but also to liquidate the debts of the *Christian Recorder*, a black Philadelphia newspaper started in 1852 and to which Fanny Jackson often contributed articles concerning the need for industrial education. The newspaper had become an important part of the black community and Ms. Jackson felt that it must be preserved "to keep open an honorable vocation to colored men." It was during one of these fundraising efforts that she met the Reverend Levi J. Coppin, a minister in the AME church, whom she married in December of 1881. She refused, however, to give up her position at ICY. Even when that same year her husband was transferred to Baltimore, she remained in Philadelphia.

The next step in making the industrial program a successful one was to find work for those who completed the training. "This proved to be no easy task."[16] This was especially true for the women. To help solve this problem Fanny Coppin decided that the thing to do was to have an exhibition of the students' work, and so she began the Industrial Exchange. The women exhibited samples of their sewing, millinery, and cooking. Through the Exchange the Institute grew in popularity and attracted students from many states. Mrs. Coppin opened her home and rented a ten room dormitory to accommodate these new students. Those who could not afford to pay rent did light housekeeping at the dormitory.

Fanny Coppin made the Institute for Colored Youth a success. Many of the students who graduated from the school went on to college, many became professionals. Even though she fought hard for the industrial program to meet the need of the masses, she always remained committed to classical education.[17] She just knew it was not for everyone.

One of her students, John Durham, told of how Fanny Coppin suggested he become an engineer. It seems that Durham's first meeting with Mrs. Coppin was when he was being reprimanded by his teacher, Richard D'Reef Venning. She walked over to where the youth was being disciplined and asked his name. She chatted with him and in the course of the conversation asked him what were his plans after he finished at the Institute. He said that he planned to become a clerk. According to Durham, she mildly protested and went on to "tell me all of the great works yet to be done by specialists in the learned professions, great cures to be made by great colored doctors, cases to be won by colored lawyers, books to be made by colored writers."[18]

When she found out that Durham was an excellent math student, she said, "I think I'll have to make you a civil engineer." John Durham did become a civil engineer, and later he became U.S. Consul to San Domingo and Minister to Haiti.

The Close of the Institute for Colored Youth

By the close of the nineteenth century Booker T. Washington was gaining more and more recognition as the spokesman for African American people. His growing appeal in many ways led to the close of the Institute for Colored Youth. After hearing many of Washington's speeches on the education of the Negro, especially after his address at the Cotton Exposition in Atlanta in 1895 where he urged blacks not to seek equality with whites, Fanny Coppin was requested by her Board of Managers to "tone down" her classes at the Institute. The managers felt the classes were pitched too high.[19]

Fanny Jackson Coppin retired from the Institute for Colored Youth in June 1902 as the managers became more and more influenced by the ideology of Washington. After retirement she continued in her mission work. She served on the Board of Managers of the Home for the Aged and Infirmed Colored People in Philadelphia for over twenty years. She also continued to write for the *Christian Recorder* encouraging blacks to aid themselves. She also became very involved in missionary projects of the A.M.E. church. In 1900 her husband, Rev. Levi Coppin, was elected bishop of the A.M.E. church and later assigned to Cape Town, South Africa. Fanny Coppin joined her husband in South

Africa in November, 1902 and while there she organized temperance and missionary societies. Once again she demonstrated tremendous spirit and energy; sometimes she had to travel as far as 1360 miles from Cape Town to distant missions to talk to the women about righteousness and temperance.

The Coppins returned to the United States in the spring of 1904. Fanny Coppin's health began to fail and she was confined to her house much of the time. In the last year of her life, however, she wrote her autobiography, *Reminiscences of School Life, and Hints on Teaching*. Fanny Jackson Coppin died January 21, 1913.

MARY ANN SHADD CARY
1823–1893

Early Background and Training

Unlike Fanny Coppin, Mary Ann Shadd was born free. Her father, Abraham Shadd, had inherited from his father not only his business as a shoemaker, but an estate valued at approximately $1,300. Abraham was able to add to his inherited wealth and acquired property in Wilmington, Delaware. By the time Mary Ann (the eldest of thirteen children) was born, the Shadd's were considered quite well to do.[20]

Mary Ann was introduced to the struggle for civil rights and equality at a very young age. Abraham Shadd was an active abolitionist and served as Delaware's representative to the National Convention for the Improvement of Free People of Color. He served as president of the convention in 1833. By this time Mr. Shadd had moved his family to West Chester, Pennsylvania in search of better educational opportunities. At that time Wilmington offered few educational opportunities to blacks. In Pennsylvania his boot and shoe store thrived and he was able to devote even more time to the cause of racial equality. The Shadd home became a station in the Underground Railroad. Shadd believed strongly that black people must help one another if they were to prosper and preached education, thrift, and hard work in his home.

It was in this hearty, hard working environment that Mary Ann Shadd was raised. She completed six years in a Quaker school in West Chester.[21] No doubt the Quakers also influenced Mary Ann's abolitionist tendencies. But her father's teachings on self-help and self-denial seem to have been instrumental in forming her character.

Philosophy and Teaching Experience

After completing school Mary Ann Shadd returned to Wilmington to start a school for black youth. She taught at black schools in Wilmington, New York City, West Chester, and Norristown, Pennsylvania. In these schools she passed on her belief that education, hard work, and thrift were the means for blacks to become fully integrated into American society. Ms. Shadd believed that full integration was the ultimate goal that blacks should strive for. This set her apart from other black leaders and she was often the object of sharp criticism. But she defended her stance, calling upon African Americans to institute their own programs of antislavery reform and not to become dependent on white support. During this time she increased her reputation as an antislavery activist.

Migration to Canada

When the Fugitive Slave Law was passed in 1850, free blacks were in increasing danger. Mary Ann Shadd was influenced by an increasing number of black leaders who gave up any idea that blacks would be allowed to integrate into the American mainstream. Leaders like Lewis Woodson, Henry Bibb, Samuel Ringgold Ward, and Henry Highland Garnett called for emigration to Canada. Mary Ann Shadd and her brother, Isaac, joined this group, and in the fall of 1851 they arrived in Toronto.

Once in Canada, Mary Ann Shadd quickly became active in the affairs concerning her people. She participated in a conference in 1851 of black leaders who came together to discuss emigration, the repercussions of the Fugitive Slave Law, and the new environment of American blacks living in Canada.[22] She found once again that her integrationist philosophy was met with criticism from other black leaders. Lewis Woodson, Henry Bibb, and Martin Delaney, the most prominent of the emigrationist leaders, argued that integration could not work and that the only hope for a strong black community was that they remain rich in their own culture, world view, and maintain an identity based on a common black experience. This was the most popular view of the day.

Mary Ann Shadd was most strongly challenged by Henry Bibb. Bibb had been a slave. After many attempts he finally escaped to Detroit in 1842. After the Fugitive Slave Act was passed, Bibb moved his family to Canada. He settled in Chatham, Canada where he established a bimonthly newspaper, *The Voice of the Fugitive*. Bibb started a separate black day school, participated in the building of a Methodist church, and helped found educational, temperance, and antislavery societies in western Canada. By the time Mary Ann and Isaac Shadd arrived in 1851, Bibb was a highly respected and influential leader.

Mary Ann Shadd first settled in Windsor, Canada. She chose Windsor because to her the black community in this city seemed the most destitute of all of western Canada. Believing that education and literacy was essential for a liberated black community, Shadd started a private school for the underprivileged. The unique thing about this school was that it was open to both black and white students.

Henry Bibb and his wife, Mary, quickly denounced the school. They called upon the black community to petition for a separate public school rather than support a private integrated school. Shadd found that integrationism was not popular with blacks or whites. Legally blacks were entitled to attend any Canadian school, but since neither group preferred that arrangement, schools remained segregated. Shadd felt, however, that as long as the two races were segregated racial discrimination was inevitable as neither group would trust the other. Moreover she believed that, "separate black schools, black utopian or vocational communities such as Elgin, Dawn, or Wilberforce, and the Refugee Home Society alienated whites even further both by their economic failure and by their perpetuation of old stereotypes that identified blacks as incapable of living a life of freedom."[23]

The *Provincial Freeman*

The private school which she established closed after eight weeks, but Mary Ann Shadd continued to push for integration. She wrote letters to newspapers and in 1852 published a pamphlet entitled, *A Plea for Emigration, or Notes of Canada West, in Its Moral, Social, and Political Aspect.* In this document she encouraged emigration to Canada and denounced separatist attitudes. She still felt that Canada held more hope for black people than the United States despite distrust and prejudice between blacks and whites. To counter the increasing attacks Henry Bibb launched from *The Voice of the Fugitive*, Mary Ann Shadd published her own paper the *Provincial Freeman* in 1853 making her the first black, female editor in North America.

To support her venture she called upon Samuel Ringgold Ward. Ward was a prominent fugitive slave living in Canada. Ward was given the title of editor of the paper. His name was well respected and helped generate interest, but it was known that Mary Ann Shadd was the actual editor. After the first issue was published, Shadd suspended publication for a year and traveled throughout the United States and Canada to raise money for future editions.

In early 1854 she returned to Canada, but this time she chose Toronto to be her base—probably because of its larger black business community. In March 1854 the *Provincial Freeman* was again in circulation. The paper's new motto, "Self-Reliance Is the Fine Road to Independence," reflected the spirit of its editor who wrote to "represent the intelligent choice of 'Colored Canadians' for integration."[24] Shadd also used the paper to denounce discrimination and cited specific examples of racist white behavior. Her paper provided valuable information for blacks fleeing the United States. She told them what cities would be the least discriminating, what areas were safe, and what areas to avoid. She also used the newspaper as a means to spread the lessons of self-help and independence she had learned as a child. She encouraged blacks coming to Canada to strive for financial independence and thereby "prove the fitness of slaves for freedom."

The paper was published sporadically until 1859 when the financial burden became too great. Two years earlier Mary Ann Shadd had married Thomas Cary, a Toronto barber. She ran the newspaper, went on frequent trips to gather subscriptions, and when at home took care of her two children. When the paper folded, Mary Ann Shadd Cary returned to full-time teaching at an American Missionary Association school. She also increased her abolitionist efforts. She was a supporter of William Lloyd Garrison, and she befriended John Brown just weeks before his demise at Harper's Ferry. She later wrote a eulogy for Brown which appeared in the New York *Weekly Anglo-African*.

After Thomas Cary died in 1860, Mary Ann Cary remained in Chatham teaching at an interracial school, but continued to write letters to abolitionist papers in the United States. When the Civil War began, she accepted an invitation from Martin Delaney to return to the States and work as an enlistment recruiter. She later received a commission as a U.S. recruitment officer from Oliver P. Morton, governor of Indiana, making her the only woman officially commissioned as a recruiting agent.

After the Civil War many of the blacks who had fled to Canada's safety prior to the war returned to the States en masse. Disillusioned with Canadian racism, they crossed back over the border to reunite with family and friends. Mary Ann Cary remained in the United States as well. She relocated to Washington, D.C., where she thought she could be of most service to her people. She once again spoke out, encouraging blacks to educate themselves and free themselves of white benevolence. She still saw the ultimate goal as being complete integration of the two races, but she felt this could only be accomplished through hard work and sacrifice, that would prove that blacks were ready for equality with whites.

Later Years

Mary Ann Shadd Cary continued to fight for racial equality. She entered Howard Law School at the age of forty-six and in 1883 was the first black woman to receive her law degree. After graduation she went into practice, but continued to write letters and speak about her concerns. She blasted Reconstruction politics and discriminatory practices. She even tried to organize blacks to boycott all white businesses that had discriminatory practices.

She also turned her energy to gender discrimination and became a supporter of the women's suffrage movement. She argued that the ideals of the founding fathers should apply to women. In 1874 she, along with sixty-three other women, tried unsuccessfully to register to vote. Her activities gained her recognition by Susan B. Anthony and Lucretia Mott, and at their invitation she addressed the convention of the National Women's Suffrage Association in 1878. Her attempt after this conference to form an auxiliary group for African American women was unsuccessful, but still she did not give up. Until her death in 1893 she continued to lecture and write. Her lifelong dream to see blacks and whites fully integrated was not realized, but she never gave up her belief that through education, hard work, and thrift equality would be realized.

CHARLOTTE FORTEN GRIMKE
1837–1914

Philadelphia: The Early Years

Charlotte L. Forten, the "darling of the abolitionists," was born into a family of relative wealth and influence. She was the granddaughter of James Forten, who had made a considerable fortune as a sail maker in Philadelphia. James Forten was born a free man and attended the school of Anthony Benezet, a famed Quaker abolitionist.

James Forten revealed his rebellious spirit throughout life. He invested much of his income to abolitionist organizations and he volunteered his time to numerous civic activities. Therefore, young Charlotte Forten was exposed from birth to the abolitionist cause. She often sat at the dinner table with William Lloyd Garrison, Reverend Richard Allen, Reverend Absolom Jones, and others who were well recognized in the abolitionist cause.

James Forten's children all developed a passion for abolition. Sarah Forten was a leader in a national convention of Negro women that met in 1837 to press for abolition. Margretta Forten taught in a Philadelphia school, but also found time to be the secretary for the Philadelphia Female Antislavery Society. Harriett Forten was a very prominent member of Philadelphia society; and Charlotte's father, Robert Forten, was a prominent speaker, often called upon to speak at abolitionist causes. He later died in 1864 while serving as a private in the Forty-third United States Colored Regiment. He was the first African American to be buried with full military honors.

For a generation the Forten home was a mecca for abolitionists. John Greenleaf Whittier, the abolitionist poet, wrote a poem entitled "To the Daughters of James Forten" commemorating the warmth and hospitality of the Forten home.[25]

It was almost inevitable that the young Charlotte Forten would have abolitionist sentiments. She was often anguished by the fact that as a black woman she was despised by whites who did not even know her. She wrote:

> How strange it is that in a world so beautiful, there can be so much wickedness. . . . Would that those with whom I shall recite to-morrow [sic] could sympathize with me in this; would that they could look upon all God's creatures without respect to color, feeling that it is character alone which makes the true man or woman! I earnestly hope that the time will come when they feel thus. . . .[26]

Charlotte Forten's desire to excel and prove that she was an accomplished black woman was so deep that she designed a rigorous course of study for herself. Her journal was part of a plan to discipline herself. For nearly ten years she kept a journal. It is fortunate that she did so because her writings on her experience at Port Royal, South Carolina provide an informative chronicle of the unique experiment that took place there.

Charlotte received her early education from tutors because she was denied admission to the white schools in Philadelphia. In 1854 she left Philadelphia to attend school in Salem, Massachusetts. In Salem she lived in the house of Charles Lenox Remond. Remond was a well-known black abolitionist and was a lecturing agent for the Massachusetts Antislavery Society. The Remond home was a headquarters for all antislavery lecturers who passed through the city.[27] So once again Charlotte was exposed to the ideas and teachings of the greatest abolitionists of the time.

Being surrounded by so many of these great leaders had its effect on Charlotte. She wanted to find some way to serve those for whom liberty was still a dream. She decided to become a teacher and enrolled in the Salem Normal School. Upon graduation she became the first black teacher at the Epes Grammar School in Salem. Despite the general prejudice she met with some in the community, she was accepted quite readily in the school. She remained in Salem for the next two years and left when the demands of teaching drained her of her health. She left Salem and returned to Philadelphia where she spent the next four years rather uneventfully. She occasionally taught school with her Aunt Margaretta, but her health was too fragile for her to remain long.

Charlotte Forten finally found a way to serve her people when the Civil War began and President Lincoln placed a blockade on the Confederate coast.

Port Royal, South Carolina

The "Port Royal Experiment" is termed by some as the first, though unofficial, federally funded adult education project. [28] It is unofficial because adult education historians do not usually look seriously at educational projects which began prior to the early 1900's. The "Port Royal Experiment," however, was conducted with the full support of the War Department and the Treasury Department and can be considered to be the first government attempt to involve itself in literacy education.

It was decided by Northern war strategists that the two major Confederate ports, Charleston, South Carolina and Savannah, Georgia were vital strategic points. When General William

Tecumseh Sherman took the harbor on the island of Port Royal to choke off those cities and enforce the blockade, the landowners fled the island upon arrival of the soldiers and left behind approximately 10,000 slaves.[29] General Sherman wrote the War Department asking that "suitable instructors be sent to the Negroes, to teach them all the necessary rudiments of civilization, and . . . that agents properly qualified, be employed and sent here to take charge of the plantations and superintend the work of the blacks until they be sufficiently enlightened to think and provide for themselves."[30]

The War Department turned the matter over to the Treasury Department headed by Salmon P. Chase. Chase, an abolitionist, thought the request was a wonderful opportunity to prove that blacks were not an inferior race and refute the claims of the Southern plantation owners. He contacted another abolitionist, Edward L. Pierce and asked him to organize the operation. Pierce used his ties with the American Missionary Association to form the Educational Commission. He also sought the help of a New York group called the New York National Freedman's Relief Association. The original "Gideonites" as they were called, composed of forty-one men and twelve women, left for Port Royal on March 3, 1862.[31]

Charlotte Forten did not join the group until October of 1862. She had applied to the Boston Educational Commission in August, but did not get a satisfactory response from them. She then went to the Philadelphia Port Royal Relief Association and with the help of friends secured a position as a teacher.

The teachers and officials who oversaw the experiment hoped to prove two things. One was the ability of the former slaves to learn, and the other was the bravery of black soldiers in combat.[32] Charlotte Forten and the other teachers struggled to teach reading, writing, and math to classrooms often crowded with not only children, but grown men and women as well. In a letter to William Lloyd Garrison, Charlotte Forten writes about some of her adult students:

I have some grown pupils—people on our own plantation—who take lessons in the evenings. It will amuse you to know that one of them,—our man-of-all-work—is named *Cupid*. (Venuses and Cupids are very common here.) He told me he was "feared" he was almost too old to learn, but I assured him that that was not the case, and now he is working diligently at the alphabet. One of my people—Harry—is a scholar to be proud of. He makes most wonderful improvement. I never saw anyone so determined to learn.[33]

Harry was not the only one who was determined to learn. Reading and writing had for so long been denied the slaves that the teachers were welcomed with open arms. The strict laws forbidding the teaching of blacks served to enhance the value of a basic education. "Literacy was power, and the blacks were acutely aware of it. It was a necessary but not sufficient component in the struggle for self-protection and the larger struggle for meaningful liberty."[34]

Yet while Charlotte Forten was sympathetic with the situation of her students and believed that education was the means to the "uplifting of the race," she could not help being condescending toward her black students. Her own life circumstances were so far removed from the people that she taught that she felt little real relationship to them. An example of her patronizing attitude can be seen in the fact that, although she often wrote of the lovely spirituals and work songs that the people sang as they worked, she referred to them in a letter as "so wild, so strange, and yet so invariably harmonious and sweet."[35]

Although she remained somewhat patronizing in her attitude, she took a genuine interest in her students. She often spent the evenings tutoring the grown-ups after she had finished a long day in the school. She writes:

Felt too tired to go to church to-day. [sic] Some of the grown people came in this morn. I read them the Sermon on the Mount. And then they sang some of their own beautiful hymns; among them "Down in the Lonesome Valley" which I like best of all. . . . This afternoon some of the children came in and sang a long time. Then I commenced teaching them the 23rd Psalm, which Miss Murray is teaching the children in school.[36]

Her sincerity soon won the hearts of the people in Port Royal and she gained another title, "The Belle of Port Royal."

Charlotte Forten left Port Royal in May of 1864. Once again her health prevented her from continuing her assignment. She returned to Massachusetts where for awhile she worked for the Teacher's Committee of the New England Freedman's Union Commission as a clerk. She worked at the commission from 1865 until 1871 when she returned to South Carolina. In Charleston she taught at the Shaw Memorial School. The school was named in honor of a friend of Miss Forten's, Colonel Robert Gould Shaw, who died at the assault on Fort Wagner, South Carolina.

After a year in Charleston she moved to Washington, D.C. to teach in the Preparatory High School. In 1873 she was appointed as a clerk in the Treasury Department. This was seen as a great compliment to her race as she was selected out of five hundred applicants. In December of 1878 she married the Reverend Francis Grimke, the pastor of the Fifteenth Street Presbyterian Church. She was forty-one years old and her husband was twenty-eight.

After marriage Charlotte Forten Grimke no longer worked outside the home, but the Grimke household, like the Forten household before, became the hub of Philadelphia's black social and political society. Charlotte Grimke remained active by writing letters to newspapers and journals. She died on July 23, 1914 after a long illness. She left behind her journal which was a "bequest to humanity . . . which could reveal to a later generation her undying belief in human decency and equality."[37]

CONCLUSIONS

These three women: Fanny Jackson Coppin, Mary Ann Shadd Cary, and Charlotte Forten Grimke were very different in background, attitude, and temperament, yet all three shared the dream of freedom for African American people. All three wanted more than anything to see the "sons and daughters of Africa" uplifted and recognized by all groups as equal. Each one felt that education was integral to freedom and in turn each woman became a "teacher to her people."

It is interesting to note that the philosophy and ideals that inspired each one of these women's actions can be witnessed in the present discussions about solutions to the problems of the black community. Many of today's African American leaders cry out for practical education and more jobs, so they could empathize with the struggle of Fanny Jackson Coppin as she worked to develop the industrial school. Mary Ann Shadd Cary called for the integration of black and white people and denounced the caste system which increased distrust between the races and allowed no opportunity for understanding. This same argument is echoed on the floors of debate today. Charlotte Forten believed that better education was crucial for African Americans and also that those who were more privileged must serve as role models and help those others who were less fortunate. African American leaders today say that the problems of the black community can only be solved if those blacks who have achieved and prospered return to the communities they left and reinvest their time and talent.

The struggle toward freedom for the African American continues today, but the lessons that can be learned from these women go farther than any classroom. Perhaps the inscription on a plaque dedicated to Fanny Jackson Coppin by the class of 1901 says it best. It reads:

> In Loving Memory of Our Teacher
> Fanny Jackson Coppin
> Principal of the Institute for Colored Youth
> 1865–1902
> Presented by the Class of 1901
> "Her Word Was A Lamp Unto Our Feet"[38]

While these words were dedicated to one very special teacher, Fanny Coppin, they could serve as an epithet for many other young women who dedicated their lives to the uplift of a struggling people.

NOTES

1. Fanny Jackson Coppin, *Reminiscences of School Life and Hints on Teaching*, (New York: Garland Publishing, 1987) pp. 9–10.
2. Linda M. Perkins, *Fanny Jackson Coppin and the Institute for Colored Youth*, 1865–1902, (New York: Garland Publishing, 1987) p. 2.
3. Ronald E. Butchart, "Schooling for a Freed People: The Education of Adult Freedmen, 1861–1871" pp. 45–57 in *Education of the African American Adult*, Harvey G. Neufeldt and Leo McGee, eds., (New York: Greenwood Press, 1990) p. 45.
4. Dorothy Sterling, *We Are Your Sisters: Black Women in the Nineteenth Century*, (New York: W. W. Norton & Company, 1984).
5. Marian Wright Edelman, "The Black Family in America" pp. 128–148 in *The Black Women's Health Book*, Evelyn C. White, editor, (Seattle: The Seal Press, 1990) p. 143.
6. Fanny Jackson Coppin, *Reminiscences of School Life*, p. 3.
7. Linda M. Perkins, *Fanny Jackson Coppin and the Institute for Colored Youth*, p. 4.
8. Fanny Jackson Coppin, *Reminiscences of School Life*, p. 15.
9. Linda M. Perkins, "Heed Life's Demands: The Educational Philosophy of Fanny Jackson Coppin," *Journal of Negro Education*, Vol. 51, No. 3, p. 183.
10. Fanny Jackson Coppin, "Training to Become a Teacher," in *Black Women in White America: A Documentary History*, Gerda Lerner, editor, (New York: Vintage Books, 1973) p. 89.
11. Ibid., p. 183.
12. Marianna W. Davis, ed., *Contributions of Black Women to America*, Vol. II (Kenday Press, 1982) p. 280.
13. Fanny Jackson to Frederick Douglass in Dorothy Sterling, *We Are Your Sisters*, p. 205.
14. Fanny Jackson Coppin, *Reminiscences of School Life*, p. 25.
15. Ibid., p. 28.
16. Ibid., p. 25.
17. Linda M. Perkins, "Heed Life's Demands," p. 187.
18. John Durham quoted in Linda M. Perkins, *Fanny Jackson Coppin and the Institute for Colored Youth*, p. 198.
19. Linda M. Perkins, *Fanny Jackson Coppin and the Institute for Colored Youth*, p. 251.
20. Jason Silverman, "Mary Ann Shadd and the Search for Equality," pp. 87–100 in *Black Women in U.S. History From Colonial Times*

Through the 19th Century, Vol. 4, Darlene Clark Hine, editor (Brooklyn: Carlson Publishing Co., 1990).

21. Dorothy Sterling, *We Are Your Sisters*, p. 164.
22. Silverman, "Mary Ann Shadd," p. 89.
23. Ibid., p. 91.
24. Ibid., p. 93.
25. Ray Allen Billington, ed., *The Journal of Charlotte Forten*, (New York: Collier Books, 1961) p. 20.
26. Ibid., p. 47.
27. Ibid., p. 23.
28. John R. Rachel, "Gideonites and Freedmen: Adult Literacy Education at Port Royal, 1862–1866," in *The Journal of Negro Education*, Vol. 55, No. 4, 1986, pp., 453–469.
29. Ibid., p. 455.
30. General William Tecumseh Sherman quoted in *The Journal of Charlotte Forten*, Ray Billington (ed.), p. 29.
31. John R. Rachel, "Gideonites and Freedmen," p. 456.
32. Ray Billington, ed., *The Journal of Charlotte Forten*, p. 33.
33. Charlotte Forten, letter to William Lloyd Garrison in *We Are Your Sisters*, Dorothy Sterling, (ed.), p. 280.
34. John R. Rachel, "Gideonites and Freedmen," pp. 460–461.
35. Ibid., p. 281.
36. Ray Billington, *The Journal of Charlotte Forten*, p. 151.
37. Ray Billington, *The Journal of Charlotte Forten*, p. 39.
38. Linda M. Perkins, *Fanny Jackson Coppin and the Institute for Colored Youth*, p. 330.

CHAPTER 2

THE DU BOIS–WASHINGTON DEBATE: CONFLICTING STRATEGIES

EDWARD POTTS

INTRODUCTION: THE SOCIAL, POLITICAL, AND ECONOMIC CONTEXT OF THE DEBATE

African American education developed within the context of social, political, and economic oppression in the South.[1] While there were significant educational advancements in the North, the focus of education development for African Americans after the Civil War was in the South where the majority of the freedmen lived.

The need for a cheap supply of black agricultural laborers at the dawn of the twentieth century was a factor in the efforts to control and limit the education of African Americans. This requirement directly led to restrictions on the movement of the freedmen and the development of educational strategies that restricted the advancement of African Americans.[2] Furthermore, the concern for economic threat from African American laborers existed throughout the life and times of Booker T. Washington and W. E. B. Du Bois. This fear also contributed to the evolution of educational strategies that called for educating blacks for only lower level jobs. The predominance of blacks in these low level jobs in turn became the rationale to developing and maintaining restricted curricula in African American schools. Such curricula, in turn, did not prepare African Americans for higher level jobs. Thus a system was established that did not educate African Americans beyond what was perceived to be their "position."[3] It is in this environment of stifling segregation and opposition that the debate between W. E. B. Du Bois and Booker T. Washington took place.

COMMON CONCERNS—OPPOSING VIEWPOINTS

Within the African American community there have always been "dual tendencies toward protest and accommodation."[4] These dual tendencies eventually manifested themselves as two distinct social and educational ideologies whose theories were formulated by Booker T. Washington and W. E. B. Du Bois respectively.

The first ideology was represented by Booker T. Washington. He and his supporters attempted to avoid confrontation between the races and sought acceptance in the South of a social consensus that did not challenge traditional inequalities of wealth and power. Conversely, W. E. B. Du Bois challenged the social power of the planter regime and promoted the advancement of the freedmen.[5]

It should be noted that these two men, arguably the most influential black educators of the time, were as disparate in their backgrounds as in their educational philosophies. Booker T. Washington was born into slavery in a one-room cabin in Franklin County, Virginia. His mother was a house slave and his father an unidentified white man. His rise to prominence was based on hard work, for he was without benefactor or wealthy relatives. Washington graduated in 1875 from Hampton Institute where he later served as an instructor for two years. In 1881 he founded Tuskegee Normal and Industrial Institute.

In contrast W. E. B. Du Bois was born after the Civil War to a middle class family in Great Barrington, Massachusetts. His family had long been free, and he grew up in an environment that enjoyed relative freedom from the racial discrimination and prejudice which existed in other parts of the country. Indeed, his first real experience with racism occurred when he enrolled at Fisk University, a black college in Tennessee.

These differences in socioeconomic background and upbringing can probably explain some of the opposing ideologies, in regard to the advancement of the Negro, held by these two individuals. Booker T. Washington's ideology is associated with industrial education, while Du Bois is often associated with higher education. The truth is, however, neither camp was exclusively devoted to one approach to education. Du Bois, for instance, regarded industrial education and college work as complimentary, and both Du Bois and Washington were interested in developing a black intelligentsia.[6]

More importantly, the two camps shared the same goal. They were in disagreement about the means to achieve the same end result. This notion is summed up by Kelly Miller in his article entitled "Washington's Policy":

> The difference is not essentially one of principle or purpose, but point of view. . . . Disagreement as to method led to personal estrangement, impugnment of motive, and unseemly factional wrangle. And so, colored men who are zealous alike for the betterment of their race, lose half their strength in internal strife, because of variant methods of attack upon the citadel of prejudice.[7]

Both ideologies were committed to the advancement of the African American but utilized conflicting strategies. These opposing viewpoints had emerged before W. E. B. Du Bois was born and involved the work of many theorists. The Du Bois–Washington debate represented the last of the great battles between the two camps.[8] The resulting failure to reach a common strategy had many far-reaching consequences. Perhaps the most striking was the fostering of the belief among many blacks that technical and vocational education was inferior to academic education. That belief made it difficult for many to realize that the advancement of the black race required all types of education and training.[9]

BOOKER T. WASHINGTON

Booker T. Washington delivered what is now considered the infamous "Atlanta Compromise" on September 18, 1895. The address primarily focussed on issues related to economics, politics, and race relations. Little was said of education. Nevertheless, the address did impact the course of education for African Americans. It summarized Booker T. Washington's approach to bettering the plight of the African American masses: finding a pragmatic compromise that would resolve the conflicting differences between the Southern white man, the Northern white man, and the Negro.[10]

Mr. Washington believed the cause of black people would be advanced through the temporary postponement of the press for racial equality and by emphasizing jobs and education. Critics of Washington's position, however, found it to have many shortcomings.[11]

First of all, critics charged that Washington based his strategy on the false premise that an educated, skilled, and hard-working black population would overcome racism. Some felt this was a major miscalculation and that racism was deep-seated and more pervasive than Washington believed.

In retrospect, this might be a valid charge. If so, Washington was indeed far off the mark. But, perhaps Washington understood the reality of the social context of the nation at that time and judged that it was not conducive or favorable to granting parity to blacks. The whole notion of blacks having total equality with whites was unthinkable even among some of the more liberal whites who had strongly supported abolition.

As blacks challenged the white majority to gain empowerment, the emergence of hate groups such as the Ku Klux Klan escalated. With the end of Reconstruction the door was once again slammed shut on blacks as Jim Crow laws were passed in order to place severe limits on the rights of blacks. Perhaps Washington understood that any attempt to move too quickly would send shock waves through the white community. The result would be a backlash of hate directed at the black community.

Critics also believed Washington failed to recognize that his publicly expressed position would legitimize efforts to subjugate the freedman. For certain it gave respectability to the repressive tenets of the Hampton-Tuskegee philosophy of education. Those tenets required blacks in the South to eschew politics and concentrate on economic development. The position taken by Washington was also reinforcing the reliance of the South's agricultural economy on black labor. Opponents believed that it gave legitimacy to efforts to restrict the movement of African American workers and created what was more or less a nineteenth century feudal condition.

Industrial training did not train the freedmen for good paying trades and respectable vocations. Instead they were trained to do menial work and to be servants. The training received in these industrial schools was inferior to that received in white technical and vocational schools. In addition, Washington did not appreciate the rapidity of change occurring in the American economy. The industrial education program provided training more appropriate for eighteenth century rather than twentieth century America. The nation was moving toward an era where mass production would require skills different from those of the small craftsmen and entrepreneurs of old. Washington also failed to see that mechanical farming and consolidation would eliminate the need for a large agricultural labor force.[12]

Washington, furthermore, failed to appreciate fully that the white supporters of industrial education visioned it as a way to socialize African Americans into accepting a subordinate social role in the New South. Washington, in accepting the values of Samuel Armstrong, the founder of Hampton Institute, unwittingly strengthened the cause of those who sought to repress the freedmen.

Perhaps the most serious criticism of Washington is his attempt to stifle dissenting voices and totally monopolize leadership. The monopoly prevented those with different points of view from working effectively in their own way while Washington continued his work. Consequently no consensus emerged among African American people on the critical issues facing the race as a whole. This in turn prevented the notion of shared leadership and responsibility from becoming a tradition in the African American community.

BOOKER T. WASHINGTON: CONTRIBUTIONS TO ADULT EDUCATION

While the shortcomings of Booker T. Washington's beliefs are often of great concern to critics, these beliefs, in fact, resulted in programs that did produce some positive results. Washington's contributions to adult education, in particular, should not go unmentioned. While he is most often recognized as an African American leader, spokesman, and educator it should be noted that his educational focus was what would today be considered adult education. For example, Washington helped to pioneer the concept of extension courses as a means of bringing needed information to the masses.[13]

Washington was also one of the first educators to advocate teaching the black masses outside of the classroom.[14] He and George Washington Carver developed the concept of the movable school. Through the moveable school project Washington was able to send instructors all over Alabama to teach the men and women such things as seed selection, crop rotation, animal husbandry, tool repair, and food preparation.[15] This kind of practical, applied educational program for the rural people was the forerunner of the present day cooperative extension. Even today cooperative extension constitutes a sizable component of adult education programming.

Washington's admonition for blacks to place their buckets where the people find themselves was good counsel in itself.[16] Unfortunately it was tainted with the regressive nature of the industrial training model pioneered by Samuel Armstrong. Yet, in spite of this, Tuskegee Institute remains today a lasting reminder of the vision of Booker T. Washington. Tuskegee has a proud tradition and it has provided African American young men and women an opportunity to learn, achieve, and hope. Washington's belief in self-help and service is relevant in today's black community.

In later years, Washington himself recognized the shortcomings of some of the core tenets of his philosophy. He saw that his emphasis on racial pride and self-help through economic and moral development fell short of a solution to the problem of racism and discrimination and that his notion of interracial harmony and goodwill as prerequisites to Negro advancement did little to address the issue of racial inequality and inequity. As a result, Washington became more vocal about racial inequality. His change in approach resulted in actions that were seen by some as being the exact opposite of some of the more covert actions he had previously taken to combat disenfranchisement and racism.[17]

WILLIAM EDWARD BURGHARDT DU BOIS

In W. E. B. Du Bois' eyes education was essential for a Negro victory over discrimination. The central tenet of his educational philosophy was the development of college-educated leaders who would serve the masses, the so-called "Talented Tenth." Accordingly, Du Bois opposed efforts to restrict college educational opportunities for African Americans. According to Du Bois, the training of the Talented Tenth was the means to achieve social and political equality for blacks. This concept did not evolve beyond theoretical ideology, however. During the 1930's and 1940's, when he recognized that there was a growing distance between college-educated blacks and the masses, Du Bois admitted that there were limitations to his faith in the Talented Tenth. The gap between educated, middle class blacks and the black poor has continued to be a matter of concern in the African American community of today.[18]

Du Bois' opposition to Booker T. Washington stemmed from his belief that one cannot divorce political, social, and economic situations. He therefore advocated that the struggle for equal rights address the deteriorating situation of African Americans in the late nineteenth and early twentieth centuries. By 1903, the year he began publicly criticizing Washington, he concluded that truth alone would not encourage social reform, only a consistent social struggle would.[19]

Du Bois and his colleagues criticized Washington because at the very time Washington counseled patience, accommodation, and self-help, the condition of the Negro was worsening. Specifically Du Bois charged Washington with contributing to three injurious trends:[20]

1. The disenfranchisement of the Negro
2. The legal creation of a distinct status of civil inferiority for the Negro

3. The steady withdrawal of aid from institutions for the higher training of the Negro.[21]

In addition to his constant criticism of Booker T. Washington, Du Bois was engaged in many efforts to improve the plight of the black man. For instance, he encouraged the black community to select its own leadership and encouraged a "buy black" campaign.

DU BOIS: CONTRIBUTIONS TO ADULT EDUCATION

In 1896 W. E. B. Du Bois, as an assistant professor of sociology at the University of Pennsylvania, undertook a study focused on the African American people in Philadelphia. The study was jointly sponsored by the University of Pennsylvania and the Settlement House. The Settlement House, where Du Bois and his wife resided while he completed the study, was located in the heart of the ghetto.

The final report, written after Du Bois left the University of Pennsylvania to teach at Atlanta University, was later published as *The Philadelphia Negro*. While this research study was not intended as adult education research, the findings reveal Du Bois' recognition for the value of adult education and his sensitivity to the need for more and better educational opportunities for blacks.

In the report Du Bois emphasized the need for African Americans to be self-sufficient and to earn a decent living. Adult education was recognized as being essential for "laboring" African American men and women who did not have adequate skills as a result of slavery and discrimination.[22] Du Bois clearly links the problems of the African American community, poverty, crime, and disenfranchisement, to a host of other social ills. He believed race and color prejudice was directly related to the continued ignorance and lack of opportunity for many in the black community. The solution to the problem rested in the hands of no one group. Du Bois suggests that in order to come to grips with the situation in the black community, blacks and whites alike had to realize that:

1) the Negro is here to stay; 2) it is to the advantage of all, both black and white, that every Negro should make the best of himself; 3) it is the duty of the Negro to raise himself by every effort to the standards of modern civilization and not to lower those standards in any degree; 4) it is the duty of the white people to guard their civilization against debauchment by themselves or others; but in order to do this it is not necessary to hinder and retard the efforts of an earnest people to rise, simply because they lack faith in the ability of that people; 5) with these duties in mind and with a spirit of self-help, mutual aid, and cooperation, the two races should strive side by side to realize the ideals of the republic and make this truly a land of equal opportunity for all men.[23]

With this statement Du Bois clearly outlined the roles for both blacks and whites. African Americans were challenged to prepare themselves for gainful employment, to cultivate their understanding, and to work hard. Those of the black middle class were reminded that they must reach out to help those of less means. They were warned not to fall into the trap of hatred based on class. For whites the challenge was to remove racial discrimination, which would allow blacks to enter into a better class as opportunities arose.

In addition to the Philadelphia study, at Atlanta University from 1896–1910 W. E. B. Du Bois continued to be a pioneer in sociological research focused on African Americans. Du Bois was a trailblazer using empirical research and conducting surveys and needs assessments. He held annual conferences to report his findings. As a result, Du Bois applied educational techniques that are used in the modern fields of adult and continuing education.

THE AFRICAN AMERICAN TODAY

The 1990's are strikingly like the 1890's. Many people are witnessing a reversal of the gains made during the 1960's and 1970's just as the freedmen witnessed the deterioration of their situation in the late 1800's. Challenges to affirmative action and other civil rights measures are reminiscent of legal and other actions which occurred following Reconstruction.

Furthermore, African Americans find themselves falling increasingly behind in the competition for viable jobs and economic prosperity. Continuing institutionalized racism[24] and self-destructive behavior have resulted in a larger percentage of the population that is ill-prepared for competition in the new economic order, falling into what is popularly referred to as the underclass. In addition, the situation for many African Americans is more complicated today than a hundred years ago. Unskilled labor is not needed as much as before and unskilled African Americans find themselves competing with other minorities and newly arrived immigrants for a few low-paid, unskilled jobs.[25]

Perhaps, now more than ever, African American educators might profit from recalling and reflecting on the values, beliefs, and the resulting actions of these two men. Modern adult educators must look at new ways to solve old problems, but many of the values and beliefs upon which new programs will be based will be the same values and beliefs that guided Washington and Du Bois. We learn from their example that despite hard times and seemingly endless disadvantage, African Americans can and will continue to contribute to the social, political, and economic fabric of this society. These two men will forever be remembered for their great intellect and leadership. Yet, while we recall their greatness, we must avoid their pitfalls. Today's African American educators and leaders must be flexible enough to recognize that there is room for many voices at the table. As we look for a solution to the serious problems facing the black community, we must be willing to consider many possibilities and not to become too critical of those whose approach may be different from our own.

It is evident that Booker T. Washington and W. E. B. Du Bois have had a profound impact for modern adult education practices. Their efforts brought to the attention of the policy makers of their time the specific educational needs of African Americans and the challenges they faced in trying to gain equality. Modern adult educators should recognize both men for their pioneering work in trying to bring education to a disenfranchised people and look for ways to once again bring the issues of education, opportunity, and equality into national focus.

NOTES

1. James Anderson, *The Education of Blacks in the South, 1860–1935*. (Chapel Hill, NC: The University of North Carolina Press, 1988), p. 2.
2. Ibid., pp. 20, 21, and 149.
3. Ibid., pp. 44, 45, and 223.
   See also: Benjamin Brawley, *Early Efforts for Industrial Education* (The Trustees of the Joan F. Slater Fund Occasional Paper, Number 22, 1923), p. 5.
   Manning Marable, *How Capitalism Underdeveloped Black America* (Boston: South End Press, 1983), p. 227.
4. Marable, *How Capitalism Underdeveloped Black America*, p. 227.
5. Anderson, *The Education of Blacks in the South, 1860–1935*, p. 33.
6. Du Bois states the following: "These two theories of Negro progress were not absolutely contradictory. I recognize the importance of the Negro gaining a foothold in trades and his encouragement in industry and common labor. Mr. Washington was not absolutely opposed to college training, and sent his own children to college. But he did minimize its importance, and discouraged the philanthropic support of higher education; while I openly and repeatedly criticized what seemed to me the poor work and small accomplishment of the Negro industrial school." See W. E. B. Du Bois, "My Early Relations with Booker T. Washington," in *Booker T. Washington and His Critics: The Problem of Negro Leadership,* Edited by Hugh Hawkins (Boston: D.C. Heath and Co., 1962), p. 27.
   See also: Francis L. Broderick, "The Fight Against Booker T. Washington," in *Booker T. Washington and His Critics: The Problem of Negro Leadership*, pp. 42–43.
   Anderson, *The Education of Blacks in the South, 1860–1935,* pp. 104–105.
7. Kelly Miller, "Washington's Policy," in *Booker T. Washington and His Critics: The Problem of Negro Leadership*, p. 50.
8. Anderson, *The Education of Blacks in the South, 1860–1935*, pp. 4 and 77.

9. Opposition to the Hampton-Tuskegee idea was not a rejection of vocational and technical training. See Anderson, *The Education of Blacks in the South, 1860–1935*, p. 65.
   Benjamin Brawley discusses the consequences of the opposing ideals of industrial and liberal education. See Brawley, *Early Efforts for Industrial Education*.
10. C. Van Woodward, "The Atlanta Compromise," in *Booker T. Washington and His Critics: The Problem of Negro Leadership*, p. 102.
11. Albert E. Jabs, *The Mission of Voorhees College*, (Columbia, SC: University of South Carolina Press, 1983), p. 17.
    Anderson, *The Education of Blacks in the South, 1860–1935*, pp. 1, 36, 37, 47, 73, and 221.
    William K. Tabb, *The Political Economy of the Black Ghetto* (New York: Norton and Company, 1970), p. 28.
    Herbert Aptheker, *W. E. B. Du Bois, Against Racism: Unpublished Essays, Papers, Addresses, 1887–1961*, p. 140.
12. Samuel R. Spencer, Jr., "The Achievement of Booker T. Washington," in *Booker T. Washington and His Critics: The Problem of Negro Leadership*, p. 109.
13. Emmett J. Scott and Lyman Beecher Stowe, *Booker T. Washington: Builder of a Civilization*, (Garden City, NJ: Doubleday, Page and Company, 1916), p. 72.
14. Felix James, "Booker T. Washington and George Washington Carver: A Tandem of Adult Educators at Tuskegee," in *Education of the African American Adult*, (New York: Greenwood Press, 1990), p. 61.
15. LaVerne Gyant, "Contributions to Adult Education: Booker T. Washington, George Washington Carver, Alain L. Locke and Ambrose Caliver," *Journal of Black Studies*, Vol., 19, No. 1 (September, 1988), p. 100.
16. Carter G. Woodson cites examples of business opportunities that African Americans have passed up but that other racial and ethnic groups have seized. See Carter G. Woodson, *The Mis-education of the Negro*, (Nashville: Winston-Derek Publishers, Inc., 1990), pp. 27–28.
17. Samuel R. Spencer Jr., "The Achievement of Booker T. Washington," in *Booker T. Washington and His Critics: The Problem of Negro Leadership*, pp. 106–108.
    See also: Adib M. Rashad, "The Pragmatic Booker T. Washington," *Muslim Journal* (June 26, 1987), pp. 6 and 30.
18. Broderick, "The Fight Against Booker T. Washington," pp. 46–47.

The term "Talented Tenth" was first used in 1896 by Henry L. Morehouse. See Anderson, *The Education of Blacks in the South, 1860–1935*, p. 243.

See also: "The Talented Tenth," in *Writings of W. E. B. Du Bois in Non-Periodical Literature Edited By Others*, Compiled and Edited by Herbert Aptheker (Millwood, New York: Krause-Thomson Organization Limited, 1982) pp. 17–29.

19. Booker T. Washington, *The Story of My Life and Work* (New York: Negro University Press, 1900), p. ix.

Saunder Redding, "The Souls of Black Folk': Du Bois' Masterpiece Lives On," *Black Titan: W. E. B. Du Bois, An Anthology by the Editors of Freedomways*.

20. W. E. B. Du Bois, *The Souls of Black Folk: Essays and Sketches*, (Chicago: A. C. McClug and Co., 1903), pp. 48–49.

21. Allen B. Ballard, *The Education of Black Folk*, (New York: Harper and Row, Publishers, 1973), p. 65.

22. W. E. B. Du Bois, *The Philadelphia Negro*, (Boston: Ginn and Co., 1899). pp. xiii and 97.

23. Ibid., p. 389.

24. Institutional racism, also called structural discrimination, is defined by St. Clair Drake as "Situations where, although there may not be deliberate intent to act in an unfavorable discriminatory fashion, the objective result of various actions is reinforcement of subordination and control over a racial group and an inequitable distribution of power and prestige." McKenzie May Evans, "Educational Strategies for the 90's," *The State of Black America*, p. 101.

25. For a good brief discussion see "America's Wasted Blacks," *The Economist* (March 30, 1991), pp. 11–21.

CHAPTER 3

MARCUS GARVEY: AFRICENTRIC ADULT EDUCATION FOR SELFETHNIC RELIANCE

SCIPIO A.J. COLIN, III

Publishers Note: *The term* **African Ameripean** *and other terms in this chapter are reflective of the Africentric perspective as held by this author. They are not condoned by the publisher and have been used at the insistence of the author. The publisher thought it best to let the reader decide on the terms' applicability.*

ABSTRACT

This chapter focuses on Marcus Garvey's philosophy of adult education, education for selfethnic reliance. Garvey's philosophical constructs acknowledged the existence of racism and reflected an understanding of its sociopsychological impact upon the African Ameripean race. It was within the framework of the Theory of Selfethnic Reflectors, and based upon the socioeducational philosophy of selfethnic pride and reliance, that Garvey through his organization, the Universal Negro Improvement Association-African Communities League (UNIA-ACL), provided a wide range of adult education opportunities that included cultural education, vocational education, adult basic education/literacy, community development, and experiential learning.[1]

41

INTRODUCTION

Adult education researchers have not considered the possibility that African Ameripeans, in response to the segregation imposed upon them by law and tradition during the period of "Jim Crow" (1900–1965) legal segregation, developed and institutionalized a socioeducational philosophy and ideology that reflected a different world view. The educational programs provided for African Ameripeans were predicated upon the utilization of the population as a source of cheap labor. To create and maintain this labor pool, members of the race were either deprived of educational opportunities or were provided with industrial training.[2] This created controversy within the African Ameripean community with the major publicized conflict being between the industrial education of Booker T. Washington and the traditional education suggested by W. E. B. Du Bois, both stating that their educational purpose and goals were to prepare the race for a selfethnic reliant existence. But Du Bois, unlike Washington, felt that the group should also have the benefits of social, economic, and political participation, with the privileges and responsibilities of full American citizenship.

Kelley Miller's (1914) view of this conceptual controversy puts the issue in its proper perspective. His view is of particular importance, as he was an active participant, a contemporary of both and had attempted to resolve the conflict between them, and it is his Theory of Binocular Education that serves as the theoretical framework for the discussion of Garvey's adult education philosophy. He viewed the Washington–Du Bois conflict thusly:

The industrial advocates by adroit acquiescence in the political and subjugation of the race gained the sympathy and assistance of those whose invariable policy is to reduce the Negro to the lowest possible terms. Industrial education became a byword. In the mind of one man it meant that the Negro should be taught only to know the relative distance between two rows of cotton or corn, and how to deport himself with becoming behavior behind the chair while his white lord and master sits at meat, while, in the mind of another, it (education) stood for the awakening of the best powers and possibilities.[3]

Miller further stated that those who are developing educational programs should be possessed of "binocular vision" that an educational philosophy should reflect an understanding of the duality of needs to be fulfilled. Thus, he argued that instrumentality (hand) and personality (head) development were both needed in the education of the African Ameripeans. In his explanation of binocular vision and its correlation to the purpose of education, he states that education has two distinctive, but not autonomous, functions.

> Education is not an end in itself, but is conditioned upon the nature of man and upon his place in the social scheme; it is not an independent and self-contained entity, but is conducive to the fulfillment of ulterior aims. The pedagogical ideal and method will always depend upon the queries—"What is the chief aim of man?" and "What does society require of him?"[4]

According to Miller, there are four characteristics that describe personality development in that it "inheres in the nature of man and is conditioned only by innate economy of human nature; is independent of time, place and circumstances; represents a pedagogical constant, and is generic in its embracement of all mankind."[5]

Instrumentality development is characterized as being "responsive to contemporary social demands; is adjustable to various elements, time and place and circumstances; presents the wide margin of variation; (and) is specific in its application to the peculiar needs and requirements of each individual."[6]

Miller stressed the point that the failure of educational providers to understand the conceptual continuity inherent in this philosophy leads to an inability on their part to provide appropriate programs, which ". . . leads to much confusion of thought and obfuscation of counsel in our pedagogical discussion."[7]

As such, in Miller's view, any educational program provided for the education of the race that is based upon one set of needs (individual or societal, internal or external), that prepares the individual for inclusion into a single area of life, renders the learner nonfunctional. He states: "Any scheme of education which is focused upon specific educational preparation, without a broader basis of appeal, is as ineffectual as to substitute symptomatic for systematic treatment of therapeutics."[8]

If African Ameripeans do not possess a strong sense of the selfethnic and confidence in relating to the world, if they cannot see the value of a learned skill relative to its utility in the improvement of that world, then they indeed become no more than instruments to be used by others for the benefit of others:

> To make bricklayers men is a hundred fold more difficult than to make men bricklayers; for, if there be men, they will make bricks, even without straw, if bricks must needs be made. Consciousness of personality energizes all of the faculties and powers and gives them facility and adaptability as nothing else can do.[9]

Two years after the publication of Miller's theory, Marcus Garvey responded with the development of education for selfethnic reliance and educational programs that focused on this and economic development, reflecting this binocular vision of education.

It should be noted that industrial education was not a new concept. The education provided for African Ameripean adults prior to the 1900's, beginning with slavery, was industrial (vocational). These vocational institutions (plantations) provided the slaves with those skills that would enable them to function as slave laborers.[10] The justification for this type of education was that the level of skills taught was equal to their level of intelligence. This rationale fulfilled a basic function, but in doing so highlighted a glaring contradiction:

> The institution of slavery made requisition upon the Negro physical faculties alone, and therefore the higher susceptibilities of his nature were ingeniously denied and prudently suppressed. Ordained intellectual and moral inferiority is the only valid justification of political and social subordination. . . . Thus we see

that those who most confidently proclaim that the Negro, by nature is incapable of comprehending the intellectual basis of the Aryan culture and civilization are ever on the alert to prevent him from attempting the impossible. If the Negro's skull was too thick to learn, as the dogma ran, why pass the laws forbidding him to try.[11]

This socioeducational policy spawned an African Ameripean response both philosophical and programmatic which was reflected in the socioeducational philosophy of Marcus Garvey and the adult education program of his organization, the UNIA-ACL. A short discussion of the difference between this organization and those that are briefly mentioned as providers of adult education activities for African Ameripeans during this period, the National Association for the Advancement of Colored People (NAACP) and the National Urban League[12] will be provided. An understanding of the differences between these organizations in terms of their leadership, purpose, objectives, and educational programs is significant to an understanding of the foundations of Garvey's philosophy.

UNIVERSAL NEGRO IMPROVEMENT ASSOCIATION-AFRICAN COMMUNITIES LEAGUE

The UNIA-ACL was founded by Garvey in New York in 1918, and was quite different from the NAACP and NUL in that it rejected the belief that only through integration could African Ameripeans develop and be successful. Garvey contended that only in a segregated society, where the burden of proof was not thrust upon them, could African Ameripeans develop to their full potential. Only by doing for self could the race be successful. As Garvey observed: "If the American Negro has accomplished anything in industry, in agriculture, in commerce, in the professions and general economics it is because of the enforced system of segregation."[13] The UNIA-ACL rejected the use of moral suasion as a means of combating racism, and this position not only alienated African Ameripean leaders, but also the good friends of the

"Negro," the liberal, progressive, and philanthropic Euroamericans. By advocating selfethnic reliance, Garvey

> rejected reason and moral suasion as methods of obtaining justice, and in so doing rejected the very foundation of reform in America. Social change in this country occurs, according to the official view, through the system with the methods of propaganda, moral pressure, and education. Black and white reformers held firmly to this democracy.

Thus, Garvey's utter repudiation of these methods, his replacement of them with direct action by blacks to better their own lot and to remove themselves from white America, was clearly a stinging indictment of the American system.[14]

As if this were not enough, for the first time African Ameripeans were in the vanguard of their own liberation movement. This movement challenged the integrity and effectiveness of the two leading integrated organizations—the NAACP and the Urban League—and brought into question the motives of those African Ameripeans involved in them. The explanation offered by Garvey strongly suggested that this philosophy was a natural response to an unnatural situation:

> It may be argued that race first is racial selfishness, and as such will not remove the reasons that called it into being; (b)ut this argument loses its validity when recognition is taken of the fact that certain problems seem to suggest their own remedies. . . . To say that because Negroes are the victims of organized race first sentiment on the part of white people they should not organize along lines o(f) race first to defend themselves is to inferentially condone their present oppression and counsel meek submission to its perpetuation. Failure on the part of the oppressed to organize in terms of self as opposed to similar kinds of organizations on the part of their oppressors most naturally make their oppression more through. "Race first," "Negro First," or whatever the shibboleth adopted by Negroes may be, *finds its highest justification in the practices and methods of their oppressors.* . . .[15]

Garvey's philosophy of selfethnic reliance became the foundation upon which the UNIA-ACL developed programs that would foster selfethnic pride. The organization's commitment to this educational goal would be the first (and some would say the only) instance in which adult education programs were developed for African Ameripeans by African Ameripeans with the socioeducational goal of education for selfethnic reliance.[16] In developing his adult education philosophy Garvey was cognizant of the psychological effects of institutional racism upon the selfethnic image of African Ameripeans and its influence on their view of the world and their place in it.

At the beginning of this century there was nothing in the life of African Ameripeans that was race neutral. Their God was white; the creators of universal knowledge and scientific truths were white; the power brokers and the power holders were white; the keepers of the dream, and the providers of basic necessities were white. Physical genocide is short and quick, psychological genocide is long and debilitating. The lack of selfethnic reflectors and selfethnic determination had produced a people who are powerless, penniless, and persecuted, a manifestation of the psychological genocide practiced in America.

Marcus Garvey was one who understood this reality and the need for an alternative analysis of the African Ameripeans' life and culture. This understanding enabled him to develop paradigms and models based upon that reality. To understand Garvey's philosophy and his movement, we must understand Marcus Garvey the man. What forces motivated Garvey? An understanding of Garvey's Jamaica and his life may assist us in understanding the effects of racism and colonization on the development of his adult education philosophy.

MARCUS MOSIAH GARVEY (1887–1940)

Marcus Mosiah Garvey was born in St. Ann's Bay Jamaica, 49 years after the end of slavery in the British colonies. He was born during the period of "reconstruction," and African Jamaicans, like their African Ameripean counterparts, were in transition from a colonized state to a neocolonial state, from slaves to share-croppers. This was a time of oppression, murder, and segregation for Africans and their descendants throughout the world. The Motherland, Africa, like apple pie, had been sliced and served to European powers at the Berlin Conference of 1885. At the time of Garvey's birth, the only African country that remained inde-pendent was Ethiopia.

African Jamaican and African Ameripean emancipation from slavery and reconstruction followed parallel lines. Both went from the status of slaves to that of subjects; neither were afforded adequate educational opportunities, nor were they permitted oc-cupational or economic participation. Both groups felt the wrath and fury of the dominant culture and had leaders who relied upon the good will of their oppressors for their freedom. Paternalism was operating on both fronts; and dependence on the Euro-americans' mind, money, and sense of morality was the modus operandi of both the African Jamaican and African Ameripean leadership. A lack of selfethnic consciousness characterized the state of being of the masses.

Although African Jamaicans faced the problem of the unequal distribution of educational opportunities, Garvey was afforded opportunities for learning that were not available to the majority of his people. His father was well-read and had established a library within the home. His godfather, for whom he worked as an apprentice printer, also kept a library and understood the power of the "word." Garvey was a nightly visitor to Kingston's Victoria Pier, the Jamaican equivalent of England's Hyde Park and Chicago's Washington Park, where discussions, debates, and soapbox oratory pertaining to local and international issues were commonplace.

This belief in the power of the "word" is reflected in the con-tents of Lesson 4, Elocution, in the Course of African Philosophy (which he developed), where he stated:

Elocution means to speak out. . . . The idea of speaking is to convey information to others. Therefore, you must speak so that they might hear you. You must speak with dignity, elo-quence, clearness and distinctiveness. . . . To be a good elocutionist you must feel what you speak and as you feel it, express it in like manner.[17]

The lessons he taught by word and examples were lessons that he himself had learned by experience.

In 1914 Garvey decided to put into practice a more racially-oriented version of Booker T. Washington's philosophy of self-ethnic reliance, and he established the Universal Negro Improvement and Conservation Association and African Communities League. Its purpose was to unite the African race through an educational program that focused on race pride and unity, economic development, and the redemption of Africa. To accomplish this, Garvey sought to establish an industrial school along the lines of Washington's Tuskegee. But Garvey's program of education for selfethnic reliance differed significantly relative to its purpose and goals.

Garvey began corresponding with Washington in 1914, soliciting financial support for his school. In his letter of September 8, 1914, we see that Garvey was an admirer of Washington's educational efforts:

> I have been keeping in touch with your good word in America, and although there is a difference of opinion on the lines on which the Negro should develop himself, yet the fair minded critic cannot fail in admiring your noble efforts.[18]

But it is evident that Garvey developed his educational philosophy along the lines of selfethnic reliance and empowerment, as he stated: "We are organized out here on broad lines and find it conducive to our interest to pave our way both industrially and intellectually."[19] Further, in responding to those who criticized the purposes and goals of education for selfethnic reliance, he stated that the problem was that they would

> prefer to see an industrial school where Negroes are taught to plough, hoe, wash plates, and clean pots, rather than to have Negroes thinking about building up empires and running steamships across the ocean.[20]

In Garvey's view it is apparent that industrial education alone was a form of oppression and continued subjugation.

Although Garvey was invited to America by Washington, who died before he arrived in 1916, he still began a speaking tour that covered 38 states and lasted two years. Ironically, it was W. E. B. Du Bois, who was later to become an outspoken critic of Garvey's philosophy and activities, who announced Garvey's presence and purpose in *The Crisis*.[21] In 1918, Garvey established a branch of UNIA-ACL in Harlem, New York, claiming that within the first month its membership exceed 2,000. It was also in 1918 that he founded *The Negro World*, which was published from 1919 to 1933 and printed in three languages—English, French, and Spanish—and distributed internationally throughout the United States, West Indies, Latin America, and Africa. By 1920, it had a circulation of over 200,000.

Garvey was so successful at raising the selfethnic consciousness of the race via the printed word that the colonial powers (British, French, etc.) banned the paper in their colonies.[22] *The Negro World* was not the first newspaper published by Garvey. Between 1910 and 1914, Garvey published three newspapers: *Garvey Watchman* (Jamaica); *La Nacion*, The Nation, (Costa Rica); and *La Prensa*, The Press (Colon, Panama). Garvey's last journalistic venture was *The Black Man* published in England from 1933 to 1940.

Given the nature of society and the historical relationship between Africans and their descendants, it seems quite natural that Garvey's adult education philosophy would be developed within the sociocultural frame of race first, race pride, and racial unity and as such would come under severe criticism and attack because the goals were stated in racial terms.

In a 1921 article published in the *Washington Bee*, Garvey asked his critics:

Why not be fair and constructive in your criticism of a good and new movement? Why not support a thing for the good that is in it, rather than condemn it because you are not at the head of it? Individuals, like water, find their level. Thus the question of race development is not with the individual, it is with the measure.[23]

But his enemies either could not or would not be fair. In 1922 his critics initiated the "Garvey Must Go Campaign" and vigorously and openly encouraged the government to do what they could not—get rid of Marcus Garvey.

In 1922, Marcus Garvey was arrested and charged by the federal government with fraudulent use of the mails in the selling of Black Star Ship Line stock. There are those who believe this action was initiated by some of his African Ameripean critics.[24] Those critics included Robert Abbott (publisher of the *Chicago Defender*), W. E. B. Du Bois (the NAACP), and Chandler Owens and A. Philip Randolph (avowed socialists and editors of the *Messenger*). The United States and other colonial governments that viewed Garvey's educational philosophy and organizational activities as a threat to their national security were delighted.

What is known is that on January 12, 1923, the infamous Committee of Eight, who were also leaders of the "Marcus Garvey Must Go" campaign, sent a letter to the United States Attorney General requesting, among other things, that he "vigorously and speedily push the government's case against Marcus Garvey" and that Garvey, in essence, be deported. The signers of this letter were: Robert S. Abbott, owner and publisher of the *Chicago Daily Defender*; William Pickens, NAACP director of branches; Harry H. Pace, the National Urban League: John E. Nail, the National Urban League; Chandler Owens, co-editor of the *Messenger* and co-executive secretary of the Friends of Negro Freedom; Dr. Julia P. Coleman, president of a cosmetic firm; and George W. Harris, editor of the *New York News*.[25] It should be noted that those African Ameripeans who opposed these actions were Archibald Grimke', Emmett J. Scott, Carl Murphy (editor of the Baltimore *Afro-American*), and Kelly Miller, who stated: "It is a dangerous principle to impose legal punishment upon men for their belief rather than for their behavior."[26]

Garvey was found guilty in 1923 and was sentenced to five years in prison and fined $1,000. The UNIA-ACL raised the $25,000 bail, while Garvey awaited the decision regarding his appeal. In 1925, the United States Supreme Court upheld the lower court's conviction, and Garvey began serving his sentence at the federal prison in Atlanta. Marcus Garvey's sentence was commuted by

President Coolidge in 1927, and he was immediately deported to Jamaica as an undesirable alien.

Garvey continued his UNIA-ACL activities in Jamaica, and in 1935 moved the headquarters to England, stating that it would put him in a better position to gather and disseminate information to the race and would enhance his abilities to advocate for "Negro" rights. This was a perfectly logical rationale, for the race relative to the world was as he described, "citizens of limitations" whose relationship with other groups was based on sympathy and bonded by charity. He stated that,

[in] our contact with all peoples of the world, we have existed on and through charity and through sympathy. Isn't it sad for a race and a people as old as the world, as old as any other group of mankind, to live on charity?[27]

While in England, he established two branches of the UNIA-ACL: one in London and the second in Paris. Additionally, Garvey established the School of African Philosophy (1937) and the correspondence version of the Course of African Philosophy. In 1940, Garvey suffered two strokes; the second one was fatal and he died on June 10, 1940.

What can be said of Garvey the man? His wife, Amy Jacques, said of him:

Since the death of Booker T. Washington there was no one with a positive and practical uplift programme for the masses— North or South. Said a coloured woman after she had joined the organization, "Garvey is giving my people back-bones where they had wish-bones."[28]

But what indeed may be more significant is Garvey's view of himself:

It is surprising how those we serve and help most can be ungrateful and unkind . . . My name I leave with you the people. For you I have built up an organization of international standing. Every sacrifice has been made. My youth, money and ability were freely given for the cause. Hold fast to the faith. Desert not the ranks, but as brave soldiers march on to victory. I am happy, and shall remain so, as long as you keep the flag flying.[29]

AFRICENTRIC ADULT EDUCATION: "THE NEW NEGRO"

Garvey sought to combat the constraints of fatalism that had become the framework of perception and behavior for many African Ameripeans by instituting a deprogramming process to eradicate the cognitive and affective manifestations of racism. This process focused on those componential elements of survival. The *New Education* philosophy of Garvey was framed within his philosophy of African Fundamentalism, which represented the beliefs and guidelines for living for the race and was based upon the seven basic values of African Society: Umoja (unity); Kujichaqulia (self-determination); Ujima (collective work and responsibility); Ujamaa (cooperative economics); Nia (purpose); Kuumba (creativity); and Imani (faith). This New Education has as its primary purpose the development of the race, those "Africans at home and abroad."

The primary goal of Garvey's *New Education* was the development of a "New Negro,"—a revitalized culture, a self-reliant race. It redefined the meaning of general, religious, and social and industrial education:

This new education industrially teaches us that the Negro must depend on his own sweat and manhood if he is to survive; this new education socially teaches the Negro that beauty is in his own eye, that the Negro is as good socially as any other race in the world. This new education religiously teaches us that there is but one God who has no respect for color.[30]

These purposes are reflected in the philosophical roots of his adult education philosophy—race first, race pride, and race unity.

The educational program proposed by Garvey taught African Ameripeans that they must rely on their own initiative; that the

only limitations they had were those that they placed on themselves; that the effectiveness of white control and oppressive constraints was dependent upon whether the African Ameripean *believed* in the doctrine of racial inferiority and *acted* accordingly,
and that their negative selfethnic image, and fatalistic (defeatist)
attitude were not due to a state of being ordained by God, but
were accomplished as Garvey stated:

> Through lying teaching, through lying education, we were led
> to believe that all that was pure, all that was good, all that was
> noble, came from those who were white, and all that was de-
> grading and debasing came from those who were black. Ah,
> that lying education got the better of us so that now . . . you
> will not believe anything except it comes from the white race.[31]

But they would learn to believe in themselves, in their race, and
it was through the UNIA-ACL sponsored *programs*: The UNIA-
ACL Civil Service Board, the Universal Black Cross Nurses Corps,
the African Legions of the UNIA-ACL, the Universal African
Motor Corps, the Black Star Ship Line, and the Universal Negro
Factories Corporation; *activities*: The International Conventions
of the Negro Peoples of the World; the Women's Industrial Exhibition; *educational institutions*: The School of African Philosophy,
the Correspondence Course of African Philosophy, the Booker T.
Washington University, and Liberty University; and *instructional
materials*: The Universal Negro Catechism, *The Negro World*, and
The Black Man, that African Ameripeans would receive the type
of education they needed, education of self.[32]

An analysis of Garvey's educational philosophy revealed a set
of clearly defined educational goals: *First*, the eradication of the
influence of fatalism. The debilitating effects of this frame of
mind upon the initiative of the race did not go unnoticed. Johnson
(1918) stated that although there were those who believed that
the race's progress was controlled by destiny, he like Garvey did
not share that view, stating that,

> Our destiny lies in our hands. It matters not whether we are
> surrounded in "civilized" America by an almost impregnable

wall of prejudice, it matters not if we are only desired when war clouds hover, it matters not whether we are ostracized, stigmatized, or crucified upon the Golgotha of American prejudice; we'll overcome someday.[33]

Second, the development of selfethnic consciousness, selfethnic identity, selfethnic reliance, selfethnic unity, development of a racial code (the Philosophy of African Fundamentalism), development of good character, and selfethnic knowledge through historical study. *Third*, leadership development: social, cultural, economic and political, (The School of African Philosophy; the Correspondence Course of African Philosophy; Booker T. Washington University and Liberty University).

Garvey sought to eradicate the more significant results of the "Old Education" which were that (1) the race became more dependent upon Euroamericans and, in so doing, relinquished the power of definition regarding the race's selfethnic image and validation relative to the basis and positiveness of their selfethnic worth; and (2) Euroamericans developed the philosophy, established policy, and determined the direction of educational programs, so that African Ameripeans not only failed to utilize their ability to systematically plan their lives, but also were powerless to implement those plans when the initiative was taken. In essence, the most prominent and lasting effects were the lack of selfethnic power, the lack of selfethnic determination, and control. For the solution, Garvey directed the race to look to itself, stating "we are therefore looking to ourselves, to our own efforts to build a civilization of our own, to re-educate ourselves, because we are not yet properly educated."[34]

For indeed, African Ameripeans were under the domination of Euroamericans both physically and psychologically. As Garvey said:

Negroes, you have doubted yourselves for three hundred years; you have believed in the almighty potency of the other man for five hundred years; you have believed God to have created you to the condition that you now live in. It is a lie, it is not so; God never created you to an inferior position. He made you the equal of all men. . . . Again I say, go out, wipe all doubt from your mind, destroy the belief that it cannot be done . . . there shall be an emancipated race.[35]

No other race leader had inspired such hope in the hearts of the people since the orations of Frederick Douglass, and incorporated these inspirations (their aspirations) into practical adult education programs.

One might view Garvey's approach to education as a synthesis of the purposes and goals of W. E. B. Du Bois and Booker T. Washington—industrial education plus the demand for the socioeconomic and political opportunities. What we find with Garvey's approach to education is something that was different, yet similar, something that fit the concept of Binocular Education expressed by Miller in 1914.

Marcus Garvey understood that the remolding of the selfethnic image and the raising of selfethnic awareness would have to be a central focus of his adult education activities in order to accomplish these goals. To this end, Garvey developed an educational ideology that was based upon the reality that the mind, and the thoughts that it generated, had unlimited potential. As he stated in his Philosophy of African Fundamentalism, "let the sky and God be our limit, and Eternity our measurement."[36] Above all, the goals of this reeducation process were that of selfethnic development and selfethnic reliance.

Adult education, in Garvey's view, was based upon the needs of the race as he perceived it, a perception that was a result of two years of travel in Latin America and the Caribbean and a year of travel in the United States, giving him a view of the race's condition unseen by any other race leader of the early twentieth century. Thus, education was viewed as a mechanism for raising the racial and political consciousness of the people so that they could participate in the building of a New Negro, a new society. If we can understand this, then it becomes clear why, in Garvey's view, the concepts of individuals and groups, learning and living, are false dichotomies.

Garvey's philosophy of education for selfethnic reliance was the foundation of his activities and those of his organization, the

UNIA-ACL; a revitalization of the African past, traditional Africanism as reflected in the seven basic principles of African society. This Africentric frame of analysis is reflected in the Father-Son-Dialogues of *The Black Man* newspaper published by Garvey from 1933 to 1940, as a teaching-learning strategy. We see it reflected in Garvey's "textbook," *Philosophy and Opinions* (1923 & 1925); the themes of his editorials in *Garvey Watchman* (Jamaica); *La Nacion*, The Nation (Costa Rica); *La Prensa*, The Press (Colon, Panama), and *The Negro World*, always the theme of reciprocal dependence and an awareness of the need for an ideology which would insure collective progress; and the gaining and maintenance of freedom.

For the reader who may view this educational process in the terms of ethnocentrism it may be appropriate to briefly discuss the differences between that frame of analysis and Africentrism. The distinctive difference between Africentrism as defined and practiced by Garvey and ethnocentrism as defined by Sumner (1906), as that "view of things in which one's own group is the center of everything and all others are scaled and rated with reference to it"[37], and practiced by the Euroamerican adult educators of this period, lies in their basic sociocultural assumptions. The Africentric approach does not view other racial and cultural groups as being comparatively inferior. With this in mind and the fact that the normative standard was white, and the normative deviation was "black," we can see that the meaning by Garvey and the approach taken by the UNIA-ACL had, as its goal, the reversal of the effects of ethnocentrism. It is for this reason that it was positive, plausible, and valid.

Garvey understood the effectual results of coloring things that were colorless; intelligence, creativity, and even God. He sought to make these abstractions concrete, and in doing to to make them more visible, relevant, comprehensible, and coherent for the race. As the first student of the psychology of the oppressed, Garvey understood the effects of psychological terrorism upon the subconscious. He stated,

. . . every student of psychology knows that the greatest force of the individual comes from within. It is voluntary. When it is

absent, then the individual is but a weakling and naturally becomes a slave to the external will and purposes of the conscious
mind.[38]

In an article in *The Black Man*, Garvey gave African Ameripeans
a history lesson on developmental dependence, stating that their
selfethnic dependence was a psychological residual of slavery,

> during which time they were not called upon to do anything for
> themselves, but left everything entirely to *philanthropy, sympa-
> thy* and *charity* of others. It was this . . . that emancipated
> him. . . . He had developed a mind of dependence that still
> keeps him a mental slave, hence he didn't think for himself.[39]

Marcus Garvey did not fantasize about African Ameripean liberation and selfethnic reliance. He developed an adult education
philosophy that would reaffirm, develop, and perpetuate an inde-
pendent sociocultural race.

Garvey believed that the African Ameripeans' potential was
limitless, and, participation in the UNIA-ACL sponsored programs influenced the selfethnic perception and attitude of its members. The utilization of his adult education philosophy provided
certain psychological benefits to the learners. One member who
has been active for more than half a century stated:

> Marcus Garvey was a success in raising the consciousness of
> Negroes to the very heights. When I say consciousness I mean
> the consciousness of who we are and to be proud of who we are.
> Negroes were always conscious of being Black, but not the
> pride in being Black. I learned about my people, that there was
> an alternative, that there was another way. I believed that it
> was possible. I caught the spirit of Marcus Garvey and I can't
> turn it loose. I got hope and a way to live.[40]

The effect of this educative process upon the participants was ob-
servable even to those outside of the organization. A government
report made this clear in its assessment of the results of participation, stating that it had ". . . aroused the colored population out of

their state of dormancy to the fact that they control a considerable amount of power if solidarity could be accomplished. . . ."[41]

The evidence suggests that the conceptual antecedents of Nyerere's *Education for Self-Reliance* and Freire's *Pedagogy of the Oppressed*,[42] which are presently accepted by adult educators as the "Third World's" contribution to adult education's intellectual history, are to be found in the early twentieth century theory and practice of Marcus Garvey's adult education philosophy of education for selfethnic reliance. The education for social change aspect of adult education philosophy was advocated and implemented over 50 years before it first appeared in the literature of the field, and it was observed that "the greatest change of all was the transformation of Negroes from cringing persons, pleading for rights and privileges cruelly denied them into up standing men and women demanding those rights and privileges and determined to exercise them regardless of consequences."[43] African Ameripeans were transformed into a single consciousness, a consciousness that was reflected in the motto of the UNIA-ACL: "One People, One God, One Aim."[44]

Lastly, Marcus Garvey saw as his mission the emancipation of his race and was astute enough to know that the race's freedom was dependent upon an understanding of the major means of oppression, which was in his view the miseducation of the race. For Garvey, the psychological and spiritual enslavement of his people was created by a racist society, maintained by its legal and social systems, and protected and perpetuated by the educational system.

CONCLUSION

This chapter has focused on Garvey's educational concepts in order to provide some insight into the conceptual and ideological foundations of the educational philosophy of selfethnic reliance, and to show why these conceptual formulations are important to African Ameripeans and adult education as a field of study.

Those theoretical practitioners in the field of adult education, who have an interest, have much to learn from the philosophy of

Marcus Garvey, in that adult education for the African Ameripean must be reflective of the philosophy of selfethnic reliance,
with its focus on the development of a *positive* selfethnic image.
Given the current rate of African Ameripean participation in
mainstream adult education programs, racial improvement and
empowerment should be viewed as both programmatic goals and
participation motivators by developers of adult education programs for the race. To some, this concept is viewed as an unlikely
occurrence within the mainstream of adult education, given the
historical lack of concern for the educational needs of the African
Ameripean and commitment to the development of appropriate
adult education programs.

Marcus Garvey was to provide the type of education that would
enable the race to reject the fatalist ideology that was reflected in
the attitude that their social environmental conditions were preor-
dained by God and carried out by superior men. The development of a positive selfethnic identity was seen as the key to this, as
Garvey implored his "students" to:

> Realize that you are makers of your own destiny, you are mas-
> ters of your fate; if there is anything you want in this world it is
> for you to strike out with confidence and faith in self and reach
> for it. . . ."[45]

However one chooses to view Garvey, one cannot deny the accomplishment of his primary goal: The reeducation of the race. As a
result, the students of this *New Education* rejected the fatalist
ideology. As one student stated, "after studying Garveyism, we
knew that we didn't have to take low anymore."[46]

Garvey's adult education philosophy and practice is reflective
of a conceptual transition process, for educational principles and
programs are based upon a knowledge of what is and an understanding of what should be. This perspective frames future possibilities, and influences what is to be learned, the teaching and
learning strategies, identification of the learner, and knowledge
utility.

With this in mind, it is clear why Garvey rejected the cultural absolutism that permeated America's educational enterprises and his embracement of an educational philosophy and mode of practice based upon an ideology of race first, race pride, race unity. What we have in his philosophy is socioeducational value pluralism rather than the value absolutism of the day. Garvey's value pluralism does not place *more* value on one culture over another, and more importantly, it *does not* characterize cultural differences as racial deficiencies. Conversely, Eurocentric value absolutism condoned institutional and individual racism, perpetuated the concept of the inferior African Ameripean, and validated the sociocultural philosophy of segregation.

There was, and is, a need for Garvey's educational philosophy and organizational activities. The existing educational system, in his view, perpetuated a race ideology that deemed the African Ameripean to be inferior. This educational system was the determinator of the race's societal status. This, then as now, had a devastating effect upon the inner-axing mechanism of the African Ameripean people. As Garvey was to tell his followers:

We have been inoculated with the other fellow's propaganda—not educated, only inoculated by the other fellow for his own convenience, to suit his own purpose; (it is) the propaganda that teaches us that there is a superior race and an inferior race. The UNIA refuses such an education, rejects such propaganda. The new education that we support is the education of human equality. . . .[47]

If adult education is to meet the needs of African Ameripeans, and, indeed it should, then the adult education of Marcus Garvey can serve as a point of reference, for it reconceptualized the purpose and aims of adult education for those people who bear the burden of institutional racism. It is apparent that Garvey understood the meaning of the message of the Zulu proverb that, in "copying everybody else all the time, the monkey one day cut his throat."[48] Garvey copied no one, and as a result he was able to provide an educational philosophy that had as its goals racial liberation and empowerment.

NOTES

1. *Selfethnic* written without the hyphen has a sociocultural meaning, and is of historical significance relative to the African Ameripean culture frame. Historically, Euroamerican society has developed concepts regarding the race that has made it impossible for the status of the individual to be viewed separate from the status of the race. But even more important is the sociocultural significance that is reflected in the conceptual synthesis of the descriptors *self* and *ethnic*. This process reflects the revitalization of a traditional basic value of African society which is: the concepts of individuals and groups are a false dichotomy, for there is an irrevocable bond between the members of the race and the collective whole. Therefore, this writer's use of the descriptive term *selfethnic* without the hyphen reflects the underlying principles of influence and reciprocity that form the foundational basis of the relationship between African Ameripeans and their race. It would be both culturally and historically inappropriate for there to be a separation between individual membership and group identity when referring to African Ameripeans. The term *African Ameripean* is used because of the author's belief that terms such as *colored, black, Negro, Afro-American,* and *African American* are culturally inappropriate and historically incorrect. Any term that is used to identify a race of people also identifies a land of origin and should be genetically, socioculturally, and historically correct. *African Ameripean* describes any person of African descent born in America. The use of *African* denotes the primary genetic roots and a land of origin (there is no "Afrocan" continent). *Ameri-* reflects the voluntary assimilation with various Native American tribal societies (particularly Cherokee and Seminole) and *-pean* reflects the forced assimilation with various European ethnic groups, particularly the British, French, and Irish during the period of slavery in the United States. For a discussion of the *Theory of Selfethnic Reflectors* see: Scipio A.J. Colin, III, "The Universal Negro Improvement Association and the Education of African Ameripean Adults." Ed.D. diss., Northern Illinois University, 1988, and "Cultural Literacy: Ethnocentrism Versus Selfethnic Reflectors," *Thresholds in Education*, 15, no. 4 (November, 1989), pp. 16–19.
2. Donald Spivey, *Schooling for the New Slavery, Black Industrial Education, 1868–1915*, (Westport, CT: Greenwood Press, 1978) and Carter G. Woodson, *The Education of the Negro Prior to 1861*, (Washington, DC: The Associated Publishers, 1919).

3. Kelly Miller, *Out of the House of Bondage*, (New York: Thomas Y. Crowell Company Publishers, 1914), pp. 151–152.

4. Ibid., p. 63.

5. Ibid., p. 62.

6. Ibid.

7. Ibid., p. 63.

8. Ibid., p. 76.

9. Ibid.

10. Spivey, *Schooling*; Woodson, *Education of the Negro*; and Miller, *House of Bondage*.

11. Miller, pp. 146–147.

12. Malcolm Knowles, *A History of the Adult Education Movement in the United States*, (Huntington, NY: Krieger Publishing Company, 1977). Reissued 1994 with new preface and bibliography, Malabar, FL: Krieger Publishing Company.

13. "Dr. Du Bois Criticized," *The Black Man*, Vol. 1, no. 5 (May–June 1934), p. 2.

14. June Sochen, *The Unbridgeable Gap: Blacks and Their Quest for the American Dream, 1900–1930*, (Chicago: Rand McNally College Publishing Co., 1973), p. 91.

15. *The Marcus Garvey and Universal Negro Improvement Association Papers*, ed. Robert A. Hill, (Berkeley, CA: University of California Press, 1985), 3: pp. 410–411. Hereafter to be cited as the Garvey Papers, year, volume, number, page number.

16. Colin, "Voices From Beyond" and Phyllis M. Cunningham, "Making a More Significant Impact on Society," B. A. Quigley (Ed.), *Fulfilling the Promise of Adult and Continuing Education*, (San Francisco: Jossey-Bass Publishers, Winter 1989), pp. 33–45.

17. Tony Martin (Ed.), *Message to the People, the Course of African Philosophy* (Dover, MA: The Majority Press, 1986), p. 38.

18. *Garvey Papers*, 1985, 3: p. 122.

19. *Garvey Papers*, 1983, 1: p. 67.

20. *Garvey Papers*, 1984, 3: p. 335.

21. Tony Martin, *Race First* (Dover, MA: The Majority Press, 1976) p. 284.

22. Tony Martin, *Marcus Garvey, Hero: A First Biography* (Dover, MA: The Majority Press, 1983), pp. 54–55 and Personal interview with Charles L. James, the only living graduate of the UNIA-ACL School of African Philosophy (1937) and the current President-General of the UNIA-ACL, Chicago, Illinois, 24 February 1988.

23. *Garvey Papers*, 1985, 4: p. 131.

24. Personal interviews with Charles L. James, 25 February 1988, Mrs. Estelle James, UNIA-ACL member for 68 years and wife of Charles James, Chicago, Illinois, 25 February 1988, and Mrs. Katie Brown, UNIA-ACL member for 69 years, Cleveland, Ohio, 14 February 1988: Martin, *Race First*, and Colin, *Voices from Beyond*.

25. Colin, *Voices From Beyond*, pp. 217–277.

26. Martin, *Race First*, p. 195.

27. "Marcus Garvey Opens International Conventions with Great Speech," *The Black Man* Vol. 1, no. 6 (November 1934), p. 7.

28. Amy J. Garvey, *Garvey and Garveyism*, (New York: Collier Books, 1970) p. 27. In 1922 Amy Jacques and Garvey were married. They had two sons, Marcus Mosiah, Jr. and Julius Winston. Both of Garvey's sons live in America; Marcus Mosiah, Jr., is an engineer living in New Jersey, and Julius Winston is a surgeon living in New York. Both along with the members of the Black Congressional Caucus, led by Congressman Charles Rangel of New York, have petitioned for a Presidential posthumous pardon for Garvey.

29. Amy J. Garvey, ed., *Philosophy and Opinions of Marcus Garvey*, (New York: Atheneum, 1982. Originally published in 1925), p. 327.

30. *Garvey Papers*, 1985, 4: p. 653.

31. *Garvey Papers*, 1984, 3: p. 26–27.

32. Personal interviews with Charles James, 26 February, 1988, Mrs. Katie Brown, 15 February, 1988; Colin, *Voices From Beyond* and Martin, *Race First*.

33. Phillip B. Johnson, *The Mysterious Life Principal*, unpublished manuscript, courtesy of the Johnson Family, 1918, pp. 9–10.

34. Garvey Papers, 1985, 4: p. 652.

35. Ibid., 4: p. 594.

36. Marcus Garvey, *African Fundamentalism* (New York: Universal Publishing Co., 1925), p. 1.

37. William G. Sumner, *Folkways*, (Boston: Ginn Publishers, 1906), p. 13.

38. Marcus Garvey, "The Negro and Himself!" *The Black Man*, Vol. 1, no. 1 (December 1933), p. 13.

39. Ibid.

40. Personal interview, Mrs. Katie Brown, 14 February, 1988.

41. Garvey Papers, 1984, 4: p. 139.

42. Julius K. Nyerere, *Education for Self-Reliance* (Dares Salaam, Tanzania: Tanzania Government Publishing Co., 1967) and Paulo Freire, *Pedagogy of the Oppressed* (New York: The Continuum Publishing Co., 1980).

43. *Garvey Papers*, 1985, 4: p. 652.
44. *Universal Negro Improvement Association and African Communities League Constitution and By-Laws* (New York: Universal Publishing Co., 4th edition, 1922), p. 1.
45. *Garvey Papers*, 1985, 4: p. 652.
46. Interview with Mrs. Katie Brown, 14 February, 1988.
47. *Garvey Papers*, 1985, 4: p. 652.
48. C. Leslau and W. Leslau (Eds.), *African Proverbs*, (New York: Peter Pauper Press, 1962), p. 61.

CHAPTER 4

ALAIN LEROY LOCKE: MORE THAN AN ADULT EDUCATOR

LaVERNE GYANT

He was a philosopher, writer, critic, and an educator who "understood the puzzling paradoxes which enshrouded certain great human problems and the long range perspective required to see and understand"[1] these problems. He was a man who sought to bring the local and universal segments of social and economic racial differences into a harmonious balance. More importantly, he provided African Americans with the opportunity to have "visions that could be attained . . . a sense of belonging, a cause to struggle for . . . a consciousness of being part of humankind . . . a partner in the creative process."[2] Likewise, he was a man who had "vision, courage, intellect, patience, and resilience."[3]

Locke has been described as a man alone, personally uncommitted, who came to see in his own situation an exemplar of the situation and problems of every human being wherever in the world people are penalized for some difference entirely unrelated to their qualities as persons or their competence as thinkers or craftsmen or artists.[4]

This man was Alain Leroy Locke, who is recognized primarily for his work in African American culture and literature during the Harlem Renaissance. However, in small circles he is recognized as a spokesperson and leader in the adult education movement for African Americans.[5] Locke believed that it was through adult education that African Americans would achieve their rightful place in this society, as well as "exhibit a profound and continuing interest in their own intellectual and cultural development."[6]

BEGINNINGS

Alain Leroy Locke was born in Philadelphia, Pennsylvania on September 13, 1886, five years after Tuskegee Institute was founded by Booker T. Washington. He was the son of Pliny and Mary Hawkins Locke. Pliny Locke was a lawyer and graduate of Howard University Law School, while Mary Hawkins Locke was a school teacher. Little is written about the relationship between Locke and his father. However, Stafford suggested that Locke was greatly influenced by his mother. She taught Locke "that authors of social tone did not necessarily understand what gave them their power any more than they saw what took it away."[7] Mary Hawkins Locke raised Locke to accept his responsibility to society, to appreciate poetry and music, to understand the Negro Protestantism idea, while protecting him from feeling self-pity and helplessness.

Locke's educational experience was exhaustive and rigorous. He attended the Hichsite Quaker School in Germantown and the Ethical Culture School, established by Felix Adler, which focused on sexual purity, concern for the working class, and intellectual development. Locke attended Central High School and the Philadelphia School of Pedagogy where he wrote his thesis on "Moral Training in Elementary School," graduated first in his class, and received his second Bachelor of Arts degree. It was at Central High and the School of Pedagogy that Locke developed his appreciation and awareness of how ideas have an impact on altering the status quo, and how interracial communication could change attitudes and bridge the gaps between whites and African Americans.

Locke received his master's degree in philosophy from Harvard University, where he studied under G. P. Adams, R. B. Perry, Munsterberg, Copeland, Sheffer, and was influenced by Royce, James, Palmer, and Santayana. At Harvard, Locke embraced the themes of liberalism and cosmopolitanism. Locke graduated from Harvard with honors in philosophy, a member of Phi Beta Kappa, and won a Rhodes Scholarship.

In 1907, Locke went to Oxford University, England, as the first African American Rhodes Scholar; not until 1962 did another black win a Rhodes Scholarship.[8] At Oxford, he focused on the

African race and searched for a sense of self-identity. His experience both at Harvard and Oxford provided him with food for thought. He found himself in social isolation. Unlike some students, Locke did not perceive himself as inferior, rather he was

> convinced that in his ideas, his intentions, and his work and ways, he was not inferior, nor otherwise different from those people who held themselves to be better than he was and there were intervals . . . when he did not appear to live under any penalty for his difference.[9]

Locke remained steadfast in his intellectual pursuit, and applied for an extension of his scholarship to study at the University of Berlin from 1910–11. While at the University of Berlin, he also studied at the University of Paris, where he attended lectures by Henri Bergson, which helped to clarify his philosophical ideas. Locke returned to the United States in 1912.

Prior to his appointment as assistant professor of philosophy and education at Howard University, Locke embarked on a six month fact finding tour of the South. The tour was significant to Locke for two reasons. First, it furthered his interest in interpreting the cultured, educational, and artistic expression of African Americans. Second, it furthered his belief that it was through education and information on black cultural ethos, that African Americans would acquire recognition and racial solidarity, and become functionally literate.

In addition to teaching at Howard University, Locke served as statistician for the New Jersey Semi-Centennial Commission for the Negro and as personnel officer and instructor in Howard University's Students' Army Training Corps. Locke left Howard in 1916 to complete his doctorate in philosophy at Harvard University. He received his Ph.D. in 1918, with his dissertation entitled, "The Problem of Classification on the Theory of Value," and returned to Howard University as a full professor and chair of the Department of Philosophy. While at Howard, Locke was instrumental in organizing the arts and music departments and the Howard Players, as well as making Howard the first university requiring general education and principles of reasoning as a requirement for graduation. He also taught at Fisk University, Tuskegee University, University of Wisconsin, the New School for Social Research, and New York City College.

In the midst of his teaching and consultant work, Locke contributed to several journals and magazines. *Opportunity: A Journal of Negro Life, The Crisis, Phylon, The American Scholar,* and *Art in America. The New Negro, Four Negro Poets, Plays of Negro Life,* and *The Negro in Art: A Pictorial Record of Negro Artists* are only a few of the books he wrote or edited. Not only did he author a series of articles and books, he also encouraged up and coming scholars and writers such as Jessie Fauset, Shirley Graham, and Langston Hughes. Locke also admired the works of Frederick Douglass, Booker T. Washington, W. E. B. Du Bois, and Carter G. Woodson.

Locke's international experiences, affiliation with historical black colleges and universities, and the conditions of African Americans in the early 1900's shaped his interest in literacy, race consciousness, and adult education. This diversity of experience enabled him to develop his philosophy of cultural pluralism and adult education.

Throughout his lifetime, Locke encouraged African Americans to learn about the history and culture of Africa. He believed if they were grounded in their history and provided with better educational opportunities, they could stand with dignity, take their rightful place in society, and be active and productive citizens. Because of his experiences at Harvard and in Europe, as well as in the United States, he knew and understood how and what things were valued in society and shared them with the African American Community.[10] He believed that

> civilization is largely the product and residue of this ever widening process of culture, contact, interchange, and fusion . . . cultural exchange passed in reciprocal streams from the conquered to the dominant groups. It is not always the dominant stock or upper classes who are carriers or importers of culture. Societies have just as frequently received infiltrations of alien culture from the bottom through the absorption of conquered and subject groups.[11]

LOCKE AS A PHILOSOPHER

Scholars have written that Locke's philosophical views were "rich in meaning and subtle thinking."[12] Likewise, they have stated that, "The cornerstone of [his] philosophical ideal[s] was the determination of values and by them the estimation of conduct which affects human lives and relationships."[13] Locke's view of life, wisdom, knowledge, and diverse background provided him with the foundation to develop his philosophical views.

According to Days and Marable,[14] Locke's philosophy provided a rationalization for a new Negro culture and was written in an arcane language only understood by a few. Yet, it reflected the democratic ideas of society and focused on the education, culture, and economic conditions of all human beings, especially African Americans.

Cultural pluralism and value relativism served as the foundation for Locke's ideas on education and aesthetics. Kallen wrote that Locke became interested in cultural pluralism and value relativism when he was a student at Harvard and this interest continued to grow after his experience in Europe as a Rhodes Scholar. Cultural pluralism to Locke was "a way of life, the projection of value judgment into the milieu of contemporary problems" and "a practical model through which congenial relations between conflicting groups could be achieved."[15] Cultural pluralism was a model of action with each individual being an active participant, and it provided people with self-respect, self-pride, and self-esteem. Yet, it rejected the idea of one group having the best culture or history and being without virtues. Value relativism, on the other hand, was the "rejection of all absolutes, theological as well as metaphysical."[16] In other words, Locke recognized the value humans placed on race was fictitious and that

the real value of things, that which gives meaning and substance, lies in their possibility of providing the human with a healthy emotional state . . . The real value of race, the positive value . . . [is] the great contribution it could make to the diversity as well as the unity of the human race."[17]

His philosophy of cultural pluralism and value relativism along with his aesthetic philosophy was an integral part of the work he did as an advocate of adult education for African Americans.

LOCKE AS AN ADULT EDUCATOR

Between 1918 and 1930 several events—black migration from the South, the Harlem Renaissance, and the New Negro Movement—had a major effect on the African American community.

It was during this period that Locke began to write a number of articles on adult education. The "Role of the Talented Tenth," "A Decade of Negro Self Expression," and "The Negro Education Bids for Par" are only a few of his early writings on adult education.

Locke's early interest in adult education was based on several factors: (a) the illiteracy rate among African Americans was high; (b) a high percentage of African Americans did not complete elementary school; and (c) educational opportunities for African Americans were below national standards in all categories— teacher preparation, equipment and facilities, procedures, and atmosphere.

With these factors in mind, Locke was able to identify the problems and needs of African Americans—housing, employment, health, recreation, agricultural extension, social and economic problems. These problems and needs convinced Locke that African Americans "were ripe for varied and broad adult education programs."[18]

It was Locke's contention that "only through lifelong learning could the black man truly liberate himself from the debilitating effects of . . . racial subjugation and educational neglect thrust upon him by the dominant white community."[19] Therefore, adult education has a twofold purpose—first, to educate the talented and gifted and second, to increase the literacy and cultural skills of African Americans.

The movement for adult education among any disadvantaged group must have a dynamic and enthusiasm-compelling drive. Beyond the mere literacy level, enlarging horizons and broadening human values must dominate it or the movement will stall.[20]

Locke's early writings were based on the previous needs and concerns within the African American community and on the role black colleges and universities had in providing adult education programs which addressed their needs and concerns. In the "Role of the Talented Tenth," Locke wrote that trained educators and leaders were needed to improve the educational status of African Americans. The "talented tenth" were needed to plan and implement adult education programs which would address the problems and needs of the African American community.

> . . . enlightened social service has always been the class ideal and the code of the professions. Now there confronts the educated man an almost universal and inevitable profession of public service, with many branches, but all of them motivated by the same system of social estimate and reward. Education must meet this by extending the professional code to all types of education, and by making the study of society and needs of society the basic and common foundation of education.[21]

Both Locke and Du Bois called on the "talented tenth" to provided leadership and responsibility in communicating the aspirations, hopes, needs, and problems of African Americans. According to Locke,

> The nation, the group that has not such leadership ready at hand, or in the making, now suffers the handicap instead of those causes which hitherto were thought to be hopelessly handicapped, but which now have suddenly leaped to the fore. The cause of our people in this world is surely of this sort that has just so recently come into their greatest opportunity.[22]

The questions of liberal versus industrial education and the educational needs of African Americans were discussed in "Negro Education Bids for Par." On the theme of liberal versus industrial education, Locke agreed with both Washington and Du Bois.

He believed that they both would provide a new era in education for African Americans and provide leadership in both arenas.

> With close cooperation and understanding established between its two equally important wings, we can optimistically look forward to a new era in Negro education. . . . We shall then see the education of the Negro not as a conflict between two programs or types, but as a mutually supplementary program of collegiate professional education on the one hand, and of the collegiate economic, technical and agricultural training on the other, with the field of teach[ing] and social service training divided between them. . . .[23]

In discussing the needs for African American education and racially separated education, he wrote of:

> the need for more positive and favorable conditions for the expression and cultivation of the developing race spirit. . . . Negro education . . . ought to be free to develop its own racial interests and special aims for both positive and compensatory reasons . . . racial separation presents . . . a negative and irritating challenge or disparagement instead of a welcome and inspiring challenge . . . this type of education constantly reminds Negro[s] . . . of the unpleasant side of the race problem, instead of utilizing it as a positive factor. . . .[24]

Continuing on this theme, Locke recognized that black colleges and universities have a responsibility in educating African Americans for leadership roles which would provide them with skills and education necessary to aid in transforming "segregated centers of Negro professional education into . . . centers of Negro culture," and in helping them "to attain their full spiritual growth and influence, and function actively in general race development."[25] Thus, he suggested the goal of black colleges and universities

> should be the development of racially inspired and devoted professional class with group service as their integrating ideal. Certainly the least that can be expected and demanded of sepa-

rately organized Negro college education is that in the formative period of life the prevailing contacts should be with the positive rather that the negative aspects of race, and that race feeling of a constructive sort should be stimulating and compensating elements in the system of education.[26]

In order for African Americans to receive the education they needed and for black colleges and universities to offer positive educational programs, more support was needed from private, public, and state institutions:

The improvement of Negro education is overwhelmingly a public task and responsibility: never for any reason or temporary advantage or special appeal must it be allowed to assume in the public mind the aspect of a special responsibility, a private enterprise, or a philanthropic burden. Many a well-intentioned friend of Negroes and of educational progress still think of Negro education largely in terms of something special and private rather than something basically standard and public, but by right insistence the public conception in this regard must be brought to par.[27]

ALAIN LOCKE AND THE AMERICAN ASSOCIATION OF ADULT EDUCATION

Locke's interest in adult education took another turn with the arrival of an invitation from F. P. Keppel, president of the Carnegie Foundation, to serve as a delegate to the first conference on adult education. His early involvement in adult education found him serving as consultant to the Carnegie Foundation in studying the needs of adults, particularly African Americans, and in the formation of the American Association of Adult Education (AAAE), which he later served as president. From 1924 until his death, Locke was an active member and participant in organizations concerned with issues regarding education and race relations.

As an ardent supporter of the New Deal, Locke believed that

the New Deal programs were "a fulfillment of the democratic
ethos, particularly for the disadvantaged minority."[28] One emphasis of the New Deal programs was to provide jobs for writers,
teachers, and artists, and to eradicate illiteracy, especially among
African Americans.

As a member of AAAE, Locke encouraged members

> to extend the idea and facilities of adult education . . . through-
> out the country . . . [to] promote the advancement of the basic
> adult education that adults can, should, and must learn continu-
> ously, not only for their own individual growth and develop-
> ment, but for society's social health and betterment.[29]

He also reminded them that, "Adult education's main objective
and obligation is the democratic extension of opportunity for
learning to the people."[30]

Locke continued to encourage his colleagues to be open minded
in their perspective and understanding of the experiences, issues,
and needs of minority groups. Thus, adult educators would promote unity and cultivate respect for

> differences and intelligent interest in group achievement and
> backgrounds and through preaching and protecting reciprocity
> instead of regimentation. If this is true, adult educators will be
> well advised in taking full account of the interests and problems
> of minority groups and in utilizing them to stimulate the pro-
> cesses of education.[31]

Like Freire and Lindeman, Locke believed that adult educators
should: (a) realize the importance of teaching people about their
own history and culture; (b) recognize and keep in mind the vital,
concrete, and particular interest of adults; and (c) recognize adult
education's role in social and mass education.[32] He reminded
adult educators that they

> have not progressed very far toward better social integration,
> or saner social understanding, or more healthy social participa-
> tion throughout objective study of history and sociology and

abstract political science. Nor have we promoted unity or tolerance by our educational policy of ignoring differences and stressing conformity. Indifference and even active intolerance have been the usual results of this procedure.[33]

On the issue of social education, he stated:

Social education is for democratic living, for squaring democratic practice with democratic theory and values. [It] will become a crusade, enlisting the common loyalty and effort of all of us, or certainly all intelligent enough to realize the significance of the situation and its critical demand.[34]

On mass education he wrote:

Mass education or fold education . . . is the democratic widening of all sorts of educative opportunities and experiences for more and more people over greater areas not only of knowledge and skills but for effective self-knowledge and understanding.[35]

Locke believed that adult educators who were concerned with these issues, "provided the strongest and most effective motivations for participation in adult education programs."[36]

In 1946, Locke was elected president of AAAE. His inaugural address called for:

an examination of the principles of adult education and stressed the need for self-criticism among practitioners. . . . He cautioned against augmentation in the adult education movement, an approach . . . he felt would stifle creative planning of programs and eventually lead to the abolition of the traditionally democratic character of the adult education field. . . . He perceived that . . . a new education philosophy would require adult education programs to be linked to the changing needs of a national, as well as international society. . . . The ultimate goal of adult education . . . was to create an enlightened society through continuing educative efforts and experiences for the adult population.[37]

The 1945 issue of the *Journal of Negro Education* was devoted to various adult education programs offered in the African American community. It was in this issue that Locke criticized some adult educators for how they define adult education:

> Anything that systematically contacts adults, almost all varieties of organized propaganda, with the possible exception of religion and commercial advertising, seems in the judgment of far too many to be . . . considered "adult education."[38]

Locke gave his own definition of adult education as:

> The systematic training of adults rather than mere informing, persuading, entertaining or propagandizing of adults is the proper scope of any adult education worthy of the name or serious consideration. It should never be forgotten that "education" is the substantive and thus the substance of the matter, and "adult" merely the adjectival reference. Adult educative effort may be as informal, as uncertificated, as untechnical as permitted by the character of the subject matter, as many-sided as life experience . . . but it must at least be systematic, standardized and expertly administered or whatever else it is (and however useful) it is not entitled to be called "education."[39]

For the twenty-first anniversary of AAAE, Locke wrote an article entitled, "Coming of Age." Subjects such as community organizations, international relations, intergroup understanding, and the future of adult education were discussed in the article.

He recognized adult education as the predecessor of community education and for its desire to stress local initiative and community collaboration as a vital and integral part of all communities.

Regarding adult education's international obligations, he noted:

> The core problem of our field today is . . . the development of the most effective techniques of mass education, bold and pioneering experimentation with the new mass media of communication and enlightenment to make them serve constructively the social and cultural needs of . . . larger segments of peo-

ple. . . . By radio, motion picture, visual materials of all sorts, the adult education radius of teaching and propaganda must be extended to the new dimensions of an international age.[40]

On intergroup understanding, he wrote:

We have reached a point of common and joint responsibility for wide scale mass enlightenment and leadership in the basic and fundamental concerns of group and intergroup understanding. That above all else is the crying need and outstanding practical objective of all informal education today. . . . To accept this challenge and be successful in implementing its realization will give every aspect of adult education a new momentum, a new and irresistible appeal, a new vitality.[41]

Locke wrote that adult education "has a new setting, a new constituency . . . new objectives"; thus "education for social literacy and understanding comes to the fore as a new responsibility and charge of the adult educator."[42] He cautioned educators that the future was going to be difficult and challenging.

Like contemporary scholars in adult education, Locke urged his colleagues to develop a philosophy for adult education which included specific and special objectives; otherwise they would continue to wander. His philosophy of adult education was presented in "Need for a New Organon in Education":

The quest for a common objective—the discovery of integrating elements for knowledge is the search for focalizing approaches in education. . . . Critical thinking . . . could make no greater headway in a single line of uncompromising advance than, with such a strategic methodology as tactic, to invade the innermost citadel of dogmatic thinking, the real of values.[43]

Locke was very active in the American Library Association (ALA). He was selected by ALA to write "The Negro in America," a study course on the history and culture of African Americans. This course was designed for use by black colleges and universities, programs organized by various groups, as well as for adult learners with learning disabilities.

ASSOCIATES IN NEGRO FOLK EDUCATION

With the support of the AAAE, Carnegie Corporation, and the Rosenwald Foundation, Locke and E. Kincke Jones, executive director of the National Urban League, organized the Associates in Negro Folk Education (ANFE). ANFE was established to

1. Prepare and publish study materials on the life and culture of African Americans;
2. Publish syllabi, outlines, and booklets for use in adult education programs for African Americans;
3. Influence a constructive program and policy in the extension of adult education for African Americans.[44]

ANFE developed several programs and published a number of books and articles which could be used in adult education programs for African Americans. Two of ANFE programs included the Bronze Booklets and a series of national conferences on adult education for African Americans.

Two years after the Bronze Booklets were introduced, Locke, in cooperation with AAAE and the ANFE, organized a series of conferences on adult education for African Americans. Approximately eight conferences were held between 1938 and 1949, at various black colleges and universities—Fisk, Howard, Tuskegee, South Carolina—and were attended by prominent educators. Each conference had a central theme and purpose. For example, the first conference theme was "Adult Education and the Negro." The focus of this conference was to evaluate the conditions and trends in adult education for the masses. Both Locke and Morse Cartwright, executive director of AAAE, were keynote speakers at the first conference. In his speech, Cartwright stressed the fact that AAAE was interested in improving programs for African Americans and that he was committed to the idea that adult education could provide the means for a democratic society:

Without adult education, no true democracy; without democracy no true adult education. The development of the education and understanding of the individual through free exercise of his will and his intellectual attainment formed the cornerstone upon which democratic government is based.[45]

Locke questioned whether or not African Americans should have adult education designed specifically for them. He disagreed with the idea of separate and specific types of education for African Americans.

The outcomes and recommendations from the first conference were: (a) adult education should make an effort to sponsor and encourage community-based forums; (b) efforts should be made to relate to the education programs of all agencies and organizations to the press; (c) adult education training should be offered to all educators; (d) an abundance of simplified materials should be made available in all areas of adult education; and (e) integration of African Americans into all phases of American culture would be a positive outcome of adult education programs.[46]

During the second Conference on Adult Education for African Americans, Locke's speech was entitled, "Popularized Literature"; he addressed the perceived needs in adult education for African Americans. He emphasized the use of visual aids in classes, and the need for educators to be informed of the characteristics and culture of African Americans. Locke also emphasized the need for basic teaching and reading materials for learners who were illiterate or had learning disabilities. The "People's Library," which included a variety of materials, progressive points of view, and general subject matter, was one means of popularizing literature for African Americans. At the end of the second conference, Locke was a prominent figure in organizing and implementing the annual conferences and was elected conference president.

The conferences on Adult Education and the Negro highlighted interracial planning and participation, brought into light the needs and interest for adult education for African Americans, and highlighted Locke's role as leading advocate for adult education opportunities for African Americans.

ADULT EDUCATION FOR THE AFRICAN
AMERICAN COMMUNITY

Because African Americans had been deprived of social, economic, and cultural opportunities and contact, Locke agreed with
his contemporaries Ambrose Caliver and Ira Reid that it was
important that adult education programs be made available to the
African American community. They also believed that through
lifelong learning African Americans would be liberated, undergo
major improvement, and exhibit an interest in their intellectual
and cultural development. According to Reid,

> The arts, crafts and skills, the music, dances, customs, and
> folkways that characterize and identify Black life are real and
> genuine. Their importance in the national cultural must be real-
> ized both by Negroes and whites. Achieving their realization is
> one of the first steps in a group adult education program. It is
> the high road on which the Negro will be made to see himself
> and will cause others to see him as an integral part of the
> American scene, proud of his cultural contributions.[47]

Locke agreed with this to a point. His philosophy of adult
education was based on the fact that all programs should be the
same; however, there should be opportunity for adaptations for
different groups and individuals based on background, resources,
and individual differences. Locke encouraged adult educators to
organize programs for African Americans around their culture,
problems and needs, and experiences in America. He explained:

> Cultural activities and their special appeals and incentives en-
> hance the self-respect of the people and enable them to assert
> themselves in healthy fashion in their social and economic
> group life, urging them on toward transformation of their social
> and economic conditions to constantly rising levels of security
> and opportunity. . . . [An adult education program] . . . to be
> educationally sound and effective must be kept from the ex-
> tremes of racial chauvinism. We must play rather than blow or

toot the racial horn. That means that, at bottom, the racial element must be factually based and soberly balanced instead of childishly, emotionally, or violently partisan.[48]

This idea was furthered in the "Lessons of Negro Adult Education," where Locke discussed what he believed was a proper adult education program for African Americans and the magnet to getting them interested in these programs. First, he suggested adult educators center programs around the culture, social, and personal needs of African Americans, while maintaining the basic objectives of adult education.

The second suggestion for a proper adult education was found in "Types of Adult Education—The Intellectual Interest of Negroes." In this article, Locke stated that:

I myself am convinced that the key to an intellectual interest is a strong emotional drive and that in Negro adult education we should boldly capitalize the motivation of racial interest and let the bogey of propaganda be hanged . . . this means we can get desirable results of serious sustained interest and effort.[49]

He suggested that adult educators use the word "race," as a focus point to generate and sustain the interest of African Americans.

The task of adult educationalist, as I see it, lies in discovering and using ways to generate serious and sustained interest. For the Negro, the one word, "race," with all its mental associations, is a tragically magic charm that instantly evokes dead serious thought. Provided we do not overwork the appeal of this charm, this special interest in the Negro, I believe that we have in it a positive focusing point for mass adult education.[50]

At the same time, Locke reminded adult educators to play down the negative aspects and stereotypes of African Americans and concentrate on providing them with the opportunities to participate within the system.

Around the mid-1940's, Locke started to assess adult education programs for African Americans. Results of the assessment found: (1) programs were inadequate and inequitable, segregated in public programs of adult training; and (2) programs were amateurish and dangerously propagandist and chauvinistic.

> This means that the Negro . . . receives least adult education, when he obviously needs proportionately more because of his minority handicaps. . . . He receives only rudimentary types of adult education service instead of the full complement of a modern program. . . . Most of what little he gets is tainted psychologically with racial segregation, which, when off set by Negro controlled and initiated projects is frequently too narrow as well as amateurishly administered. Added to this, some of these latter programs are too overtly propagandist to be soundly or objectively education.[51]

As a result of the assessment, Locke suggested that future programs be integrated. It was his vision that all special and separate programs would be included in general and basic adult education programs. He believed that integrated programs were in the basic interest and provided "the most . . . educative common aspect of the whole experience."[52] Some successful integrated programs were sponsored by unions, public housing communities, YWCA, settlement houses, and student and church organizations. These integrated programs illustrated that common objectives and interest could bridge the segregation gap. Therefore, Locke believed that:

> [T]he adult education movement among Negroes cannot maintain itself reasonably or effectively as a separate or special program. . . . Even with its body in the fetters of a segregated set-up, it must maintain a grasp on universal values and address itself beyond the narrow racial constituency to a general social and cultural service, and finally, it must align itself with more progressive programs of educational reform and social reconstruction.[53]

Locke also praised African American organizations which offered adult education programs due to historical necessity. Keeping this in mind, he believed it "must be as important for others to know about the history and contributions of the Negro as for the Negro himself. . . . Similarly the cause of minority rights is . . . absorbed in mixed group organizations with common interest objectives. . . .[54]

CONCLUSIONS

From "The New Negro" to his final work on *The Negro and American Culture*, Locke raised the consciousness of African Americans, encouraged them to study and be proud of their culture and history, and to use their creativity and intelligence to develop adult education programs for their community. Throughout his career, Locke utilized every opportunity to develop, refine, and communicate his philosophical ideas along with the issues concerning adult education for African Americans.

NOTES

1. "Passing of Alain Locke," *Phylon* 15 (1954) p. 245.
2. *Ibid.*, p. 249.
3. Everett A. Days, "Alain Leroy Locke (1886–1954): Pioneer in Adult Education and Catalyst in the Adult Education Movement for Black Americans" (Ed.D diss., North Carolina State University at Raleigh).
4. Eugene C. Holmes, "Alain Leroy Locke: A Sketch," *Phylon* 20 (1959) p. 84.
5. Days, "Alain Leroy Locke," p. 10; Robert C. Hayden and Eugene E. Du Bois, "Drum Major for Black Adult Education: Alain L. Locke," *Western Journal of Black Studies* 1 (December, 1977) pp. 293–296.
6. Days, "Alain Leroy Locke," p. 10
7. Douglas K. Stafford, "Alain Locke: The Child, the Man, and the People," *Journal of Negro Education* 25 (1961) pp. 25–34.
8. E. Toppin, *A Biographical History of Blacks in America since 1958.* (New York: McKay Publishers, 1971).
9. Horace M. Kallen, "Alain Locke and Cultural Pluralism," *Journal of Philosophy* 54 (February 28, 1957) p. 122. See also Horace M.

Kallen, *What I Believe and Why—Maybe,* (New York: Horizon Press, 1971) pp. 128–38.

10. For additional biographical information, see: Days, "Alain Leroy Locke"; Holmes, "Alain Locke— Philosopher, Critic, Spokesman," *Journal of Philosophy*, 54 (February 28, 1957) pp. 113–19; Holmes, "Alain Leroy Locke; A Sketch," *Phylon* 20 (1959) pp. 8–9; Holmes, "Alain L. Locke and the Adult Education," *Journal of Negro Education* 34 (1965) pp. 5–10; Hayden and Du Bois, "Drum Major for Black Adult Education"; Anthony B. Mitchell, "Forgotten Leaders of African American Adult Education: 1863–1963," (Master's thesis, Pennsylvania State University, 1990).

11. Stafford, "The Child, the Man, the Philosopher," p. 33.

12. Days, "Alain Leroy Locke"; see also, Manning Marable, "Alain Locke, W. E. B. Du Bois, and the Crisis of Black Education during the Great Depression," in *Alain Locke: Reflections on a Modern Renaissance Man* ed. Russell J. Linnemann. (Baton Rouge: Louisiana State University, 1982) pp. 63–76; Leonard Harris, *The Philosophy of Alain Locke: Harlem Renaissance and Beyond*, (Philadelphia: Temple University Press, 1989) pp. 1–20.

13. Holmes, "Passing of Alain Locke," p. 247.

14. Days, "Alain Leroy Locke"; Marable, "Alain Locke, W.E.B. Du Bois."

15. Kallen, "Alain Locke and Cultural Pluralism."

16. Harris, "The Philosophy of Alain Locke," p. 15.

17. *Ibid.*

18. Gyant, "Contributors to Adult Education," *Journal of Black Studies* 19:1 (1988) pp. 97–110.

19. Quoted in Days, "Alain Leroy Locke," p. 62.

20. *Findings of the First Annual Conference on Adult Education and the Negro,* (Hampton, VA: Hampton Institute Press, 1938), p. 7.

21. Locke, "Role of the Talented Tenth," p. 15.

22. *Ibid.*

23. Locke, "Negro Education Bids Par," *Survey Graphic,* 54, pp. 567–570, 592–593.

24. *Ibid.* p. 569.

25. *Ibid.*

26. *Ibid.* p. 568.

27. *Ibid.* p. 592.

28. Quoted in Gyant, "Contributors to Adult Education."

29. Locke, *The Negro in America,* (Chicago: American Library Association, 1933).

30. Quoted in Days, "Alain Leroy Locke," p. 86.
31. *Ibid.*
32. Paulo Freire, *Pedagogy of the Oppressed,* (New York: Herder & Herder, 1972); E.C. Lindeman, *The Meaning of Adult Education* (Montreal: Harvest House, 1961).
33. Quoted in Days, "Alain Leroy Locke," p. 76.
34. Locke, "Lessons of Negro Adult Education," in *Adult Education in Action* ed. Mary L. Ely (New York: American Association for Adult Education, 1936) p. 226.
35. Quoted in Days, "Alain Leroy Locke," p. 87.
36. Locke, "Education for Adulthood," *Journal of Adult Education* 6 (July, 1947) p. 104.
37. Locke, "Lessons of Negro Education," p. 225.
38. Locke, "Areas of Extension and Improvement of Adult Education," 14 (1945) p. 453.
39. *Ibid.*
40. Locke, "Coming of Age," *Journal of Adult Education* 6 (1947) pp. 1–3.
41. *Ibid.*, p. 3.
42. *Ibid.*
43. Locke, "The Need for a New Organon in Education," in *Goals for American Education*, Ninth Symposium, Conference on Science, Philosophy, and Religion, (New York: Harper and Brothers, 1950) pp. 201–212. See also, Leonard Harris, *The Philosophy of Alain Leroy Locke: Harlem Renaissance and Beyond*, (Philadelphia: Temple University Press, 1989) pp. 263–278.
44. Days, "Alain Leroy Locke."
45. Morse Cartwright, in *Findings, First Conference.*
46. *Findings, First Conference.*
47. Ira Reid, *Adult Education Among Negroes,* (Washington: Associates in Negro Folk Education, 1936) p. 17.
48. Locke, "Lessons of Negro Adult Education," pp. 224–25.
49. Locke, "The Intellectual Interests of Negroes," *Journal of Adult Education* 8 (1935–36) p. 352.
50. *Ibid.*
51. Locke, "Areas of Extension," pp. 454–55.
52. *Ibid*, p. 455.
53. *Findings, First Conference.*
54. Locke, "Areas of Extension."

CHAPTER 5

THE AMERICAN ASSOCIATION OF ADULT EDUCATION AND THE EXPERIMENTS IN AFRICAN AMERICAN ADULT EDUCATION

TALMADGE C. GUY

INTRODUCTION

Negro intellectuals in America can be distinguished from their white counterparts by the fact that the former have a grievance that is specific, obvious and constant while that of the latter is only occasionally defined in a characteristic way. The character of this difference and its implications for involvement in social movements can be understood by an examination of concrete instances in which Negro and white intellectuals have engaged in organized efforts to redress the balance between constituent social groupings.

—Wilson Record[1]

Education has traditionally been a highly valued affair among African Americans. The commitment to education has been supported by the idea that becoming educated can provide a way of overcoming the bigotry and racism that daily confronts African Americans. Yet, even the best educated African American encounters prejudice because of his or her color. As one observer has commented, "[African Americans] will have to work harder and do better, yet the result may be less recognition and reward."[2] As true as this is today, how much truer was it during the pre-civil rights era. In a time when legalized segregation was a fact of life for African Americans, those who achieved the pinnacle of educational preparation nonetheless were faced with the reality of color in America—to be other than white is to be regarded as inferior by even the best-intentioned whites.

It is this reality that sets the context for the discussion of two African American adult education projects sponsored by the American Association of Adult Education (AAAE) during the 1930s. The so-called "Negro experiments" in adult education were funded by the Carnegie Corporation under the auspices of the AAAE. An outgrowth of these experiments was a short-lived organization, the Associates in Negro Folk Education. The purpose of this chapter is to describe the context in which these projects emerged, the purpose and objectives of the projects, and the implications for understanding how African American adult education projects conducted within predominately white organizations are controlled by aims and purposes of white structures.

A brief description of the adult education movement in the United States will be given, followed by a discussion of the role of the Carnegie Corporation in shaping African American adult education projects, and a general description of the Harlem and Atlanta experiments in adult education as well as the Associates in Negro Folk Education (ANFE). The chapter will conclude with a discussion of the problems and opportunities which these projects encountered.

THE ADULT EDUCATION MOVEMENT AND "NEGRO" ADULT EDUCATION

In 1926, the American Association of Adult Education (AAAE) was founded as a result of the efforts of the Carnegie Corporation to organize and develop adult education in the United States. Long involved in educational philanthropy, the Carnegie Corporation (the Corporation), under the leadership of Frederick Keppel, organized the AAAE to provide an umbrella under which a wide variety of adult education activities were supported or encouraged.[3] In this effort, the Corporation was guided by the idea of the "diffusion of knowledge," which meant that adult education was seen as a way to make available to the general public the growing store of specialized, technical, and/or scientific knowledge in society.[4]

This was a very large and vague mission, and it needed shaping and definition. Conceived in this way, adult education was very broad. What knowledge was to be disseminated? What forms of education were most effective for adults? Were there particular institutions in society that were best suited to accomplish this? These and a myriad of other questions were to be answered. Adult education needed direction and definition. Consequently, the early activities of AAAE primarily concerned documenting, exploring, and examining various adult education activities. The product was any number of reports, documentaries, studies, and experiments, all of which attempted to give a clearer picture of the scope and nature of adult education in America.[5]

Despite the flurry of such research, there emerged no general consensus as to the definition or purpose of adult education. In fact, great disagreements raged over the nature of adult education. With the advent of the economic crisis of the 1930s, the disagreements became even more aggravated.[6] Some supported the idea of liberal education in which open-mindedness and a critical temper were to be developed. Others believed that education should be connected to movements for social change—an attractive proposition to those concerned with the adverse effects of modern life and the Depression. And still others were committed to the idea that education should be cultural transmission, that is, to become educated was to become refined, cultured, and sophisticated.

Additionally, recent changes in the racial demography of the nation had occurred. Following World War I, hundreds of thousands of African Americans migrated from southern farms and towns to northern cities. The education of African Americans, formerly considered a regional issue among leaders of the Corporation, now emerged as a concern of national scope.[7] Within the Corporation, interest in racial issues had been increasing. These competing strains of adult education and demographic changes formed the backdrop against which adult education for African Americans began to be discussed.

With the impetus growing for some kind of action in this arena, the discussions held by the AAAE began to focus on specific projects. By 1930, leaders of the AAAE and the Corporation began to discuss the possibility of sponsoring a project in adult education for African Americans.[8] The Harlem and Atlanta experiments in Negro adult education, as they were called, were planned as attempts to discern the kind of adult education most appropriate for African Americans. From the outset, however, the perception of African American adult education from the point of view of the sponsoring AAAE and the Corporation were different from the interests of the African Americans involved in the project. There were also overlaps of interests and objectives. The AAAE identified members of the African American community who were interested in the developments of adult education and who were compatible philosophically with the aims of the Corporation. Yet, underlying differences between the goals and objectives of the Corporation and the AAAE and the African American patrons of the projects led to differences in the way the projects were viewed. This will be discussed in more detail later.[9]

THE HARLEM AND ATLANTA EXPERIMENTS IN ADULT EDUCATION

Harlem and Atlanta represented two major centers of African American population—one in a northern city and one in a southern city. The decision for a northern and southern city was not accidental. Morse Cartwright, executive director of the AAAE, said that the association would try ". . . one experiment in a northern city with a large Negro population, and another, to serve as a check against it, in a southern city."[10] Given the South's history, concern over regional differences led to this choice. Harlem had become something of an African American metropolis, a center of cultural and political activism. Atlanta, on the other hand, was an island in a sea of southern segregation. One-third of its nearly 300,000 residents were African American.[11] It was a major commercial and cultural center in the South. With eleven colleges and universities, six of which were traditionally African American colleges, Atlanta presented itself as a viable possibility to test the adult education idea among African Americans in the South.

Once the decision was made to center the project in Harlem and Atlanta, financial backing had to be secured. The AAAE provided the funding with grants from the Carnegie Corporation and the Rosenwald Fund. A total of $15,000 was allocated—$10,000 to the Harlem branch public library and $5000 to the Atlanta branch public library serving African American communities. The projects, to conduct experimental programs in adult education, were to run for three years through the end of 1934.[12]

Although similar in structure and overall purpose, once in place the two projects operated independently. The Harlem experiment began in January 1932 at the 135th Street branch of the New York Public Library. One of the first decisions that had to be made was to determine what kind of programs would be offered. In the midst of an economic crisis, what kind of courses would be appropriate or needed? Early, it was decided to not restrict the offerings arbitrarily but rather to offer a wide array of courses to determine the response.[13] This strategy was in keeping with the experimental character of the project. The director of the program, Ernestine Rose, a librarian at the branch, quickly set about defining what kinds of programs should be offered and what goals were to be accomplished by means of these programs. In a report to the AAAE she noted that, in response to the growing demand for adult educational activities, the ". . . Harlem community, because of its concentration of population and its self-contained social and professional life [is] an admirable example of a typical civic unit."[14] By this she meant that Harlem was a strong community—with professionals and working class people—relatively highly educated as well as cosmopolitan.

The strong sense of community provided a basis for developing a sound and strong program of adult education. Furthermore, the Harlem branch library was a strong educational center in the community and had an established record of service upon which to build an adult education program.[15] Given this context, the development of a program would proceed with contributions from an advisory group representing various aspects of the community. The advisory committee was composed of residents of Harlem representing a variety of social and professional backgrounds. With the director, they decided policies and laid general plans for a program of adult education. Once these issues were decided, designated library staff did the work of developing and delivering programs.

Underlying this, however, were several implicit considerations. Since the Washington–Du Bois debate over African American education, vocational education programs were contrasted with liberal education as to their effectiveness for advancing the race. Washington's argument essentially was that vocational education was a way of developing practical skills needed to overcome racism. Du Bois argued that to forsake liberal education was to forego the development of the best talents in the race, resulting in a stunted development which would keep African Americans perpetually in an inferior status. If the Harlem branch library adult education offerings were to gain wide acceptance, it was clear that they should appeal to more than the educated elite of the community.

On the other hand, the government offered a variety of work and vocational education programs. The Harlem branch library's adult education program could not hope to compete with these programs in the vocational education arena. Yet, these kinds of programs had the most immediate interest at a time when unemployment nationally reached twenty-five percent. Under these circumstances, the leaders of the project decided to try a variety of programs to find out what worked. But by rejecting a narrowly defined offering of vocational interest courses, the advisory members and the director chose not to offer programs that appealed to an educated few.[16] A broad-based program that had cultural and civic content was conceived. What resulted was a conception of adult education that attempted to provide education for the masses of people by emphasizing matters of racial interest. By adding the cultural and civic component to the programs offered elsewhere in the community, a comprehensive program of adult education was developed for the residents of Harlem. Perhaps this decision reflected the limitations of resources as much as a deliberate attempt to consciously structure a program along the lines of a particular philosophical viewpoint. Nevertheless, the result was successful.

Courses, seminars, discussions groups, activities that emphasized racial issues proved most successful.[17] The Schomburg collection of materials in the New York Public Library offered a valuable resource of existing material from which to develop such offerings. This collection emphasized the value and importance of African and African American culture.[18] As a resource for the Harlem adult education project, it provided a valuable collection for informing the community and providing a basis of discussion and enlightenment concerning the nature and value of African and African American customs, traditions, and values. Topical areas included social education, economic thought, artistic expression, and race solidarity.[19]

A listing of the various activities and events offered by the program included: lectures in the park, an outdoor forum, a community chorus, discussion groups, and library study. By 1933, a year and a half after the project had begun, total attendance at all activities excluding the forums totaled over five thousand.[20] A nucleus of some seventy-five to one hundred persons who attended regularly had formed. The reports provided by the director, however, do not indicate the composition of this group. Nevertheless, it is remarkable that a sustained program with a regular contingent of participants was maintained when unemployment was high and soup lines were common. Even so, only a small fraction of the community did participate.

In October 1931, the Atlanta project began operation. Located in the Auburn Branch of the Atlanta Public Library, the project was directed by a biracial committee to establish overall policies and goals. Mae C. Hawes, a staff person of the library, was appointed director of the project.

Spanning a wide variety of topics, the courses seemed more directed to specific groups of constituencies in the community than to the community at large. For example, a list of the programs offered included: a study group of women representing various churches and denominations; a public school teachers' group that discussed a variety of issues concerning international affairs and issues in education. A relationship was established with the Atlanta University's Education Department to develop suitable material for adults who could not read. This was an effort to support already existing literacy programs offered in night school. In addition, relationships were also developed with literacy clubs in the city to assist them in procuring materials and books needed for their programs. No attendance reports were made.

Even though the project operated on a small budget of $5000, perhaps more than a little money during the depths of the Depression, it attempted to implement certain innovations in order to provide adult education services to the community. These included a mobile book fair featuring works by African American writers, classes in citizenship and government responsibilities and duties, and group activities in home budgeting and consultant services for financial management.[21]

However, the Atlanta library lacked the resources available to the Harlem library. As a result, the director sought to establish linkages with other programs and agencies already offering some kind of service in the community. This handicap proved difficult to surmount, but the resulting relationships in which adult education services were provided in conjunction with the library enhanced the quality of the program.[22]

EVALUATION OF THE PROJECTS

Very early in the course of the experiments, the AAAE determined that an evaluation should take place. Because of the unique character of the projects, from the AAAE's point of view, the question arose as to how the evaluation should be conducted. The association's "committee on Negro education" had been headed by Franklin Hopper, a librarian in the New York City central library. For whatever reasons, he was not chosen for this assignment. Instead the association turned to Alain Locke, a scholar and leader of the Harlem Renaissance movement. Locke was known to both

Keppel and Morse Cartwright and possessed the necessary qualifications. A Harvard graduate and the first African American
Rhodes scholar, Locke held views that seemed compatible with the
goals of the Association. Locke's publication *The New Negro*, in
1925, proclaimed a new era for African Americans, an era unfet-
tered by clumsy and stereotypical images of inferior blacks. Such
images represented a cultural lie. The true image of African Americans would be exposed through artistic expression by creative and
talented artists, poets, novelists, and playwrights. Through the
cultural movement of the Harlem Renaissance Locke had served
as the philosophical midwife to the young artists whose works had
stirred the liberation strivings of a generation of younger, urban
centered African Americans.[23] It was Locke's views on culture and
education that also attracted the attention of Frederick Keppel.[24]

Locke's evaluations of the project are illuminating. As if to
quiet any doubts about the need for a program of adult education
among African Americans, he noted, ". . . the decided success of
the work at both the centers . . . has demonstrated unmistake-
ably [sic] the need for and desirability of special programs in adult
education for Negro groups both in Northern and Southern communities."[25] Beyond demonstrating the need for a program of
African American adult education, Locke argued that such projects should be seen as part of a larger program of adult education
for the entire community. He added:

> Such programs should ultimately be extended to every consider-
> able Negro community in the country, but should always be
> regarded as supplemental to a general program and to whatever
> general community plan exists in the locality and should aim
> ultimately at being incorporated in such a program under local
> municipal or community support.[26]

The inclusion of African American adult education within a
broader framework of community adult education was what the
Harlem and Atlanta experiments represented.

But how could a specialized program for African Americans be
seen as part and parcel of a more generalized program for the
larger white community? After all, this was an era when segre-

gated educational facilities, even in northern cities, were common-place. Would not this lead to a situation where whites would see African American adult education as a separate enterprise, unrelated to their concerns and problems, and probably inferior?

In Locke's view, the answer lay in the need to overcome to the ill effects of racial bigotry and segregation. African American education, conceived as a wholly—or even primarily—separate function of society, had a crippling effect on the African American community. Locke agreed with Du Bois that a separate education was, in practice, an inferior education for African Americans.[27] While he did not make it clear in his evaluation reports, Locke probably viewed African American adult education as a broadly based program in which whites as well as African Americans could benefit from increased knowledge about African American culture. In Locke's view this was certainly a way of promoting tolerance among racial and ethnic groups.[28] By pointing this out in the evaluation reports, Locke was setting the stage for developing a later position in which he would state that such projects needed to be expanded. The Harlem and Atlanta programs were to be lauded not only for meeting the needs among the residents of Harlem and Atlanta, but also for setting the model upon which similar programs should be developed. Keppel, however, was not open to this suggestion. The aim for the AAAE remained as it had from the outset—to test whether adult education in an African American community would work. Nevertheless, Locke pressed his view and was supported by other African Americans involved in the projects. Eugene Kinckle Jones, executive director of the National Urban League, supported their continuance and advocated further that a staff person be identified specifically to encourage adult education programs in African American communities.[29]

Of course, the individuals involved at a staff level in the Harlem and Atlanta libraries wanted the projects to continue. But Locke's advocacy for their continuance went far beyond their concerns. Jones and Locke had discussed the possibility of expanding such programs and what might be needed to accomplish this. However, this plan went beyond the aims and purposes of the AAAE. Furthermore, the recommendation came at a time when the Corporation was planning to curtail such projects.[30] Despite the apparent good reception, the projects were terminated at the end of 1934 after three years.

A PLAN FOR AFRICAN AMERICAN ADULT EDUCATION: ASSOCIATES IN NEGRO FOLK EDUCATION

In the year prior to this action, several discussions took place concerning what further steps should be taken to advance African American adult education by the AAAE. As already mentioned, Locke and Jones had discussed a plan to be submitted to the association. The plan was reported in an evaluation report on the projects sent by Locke to Morse Cartwright. In it Locke wrote, "The new program suggested to the American Association for Adult Education with respect to the special needs of negro (sic) groups and centers incorporates two new projects growing out of two desirable elements that have not yet been developed by the three year program thus far, together with a continuing item to support some phases of the work already being carried on at the Harlem and Atlanta centers. . . . "[31] Of special note is that one of the two new projects was for "promotional work" in adult education.

What Jones and Locke wanted was a commitment from the AAAE to support an organized effort to develop and implement such programs in communities throughout the country. To accomplish this, they proposed that an individual comparable in role and stature to Cartwright be delegated to perform this function. They had suggested that Ira De A. Reid, professor of education at Atlanta University, be hired to foster and develop programs for African Americans along the lines of the Harlem and Atlanta experiments. They also recommended that special materials for study in African American adult education be prepared and published for use by adult education groups. The latter recommendation eventuated in the establishment of the Associates in Negro Folk Education (ANFE), a biracial organization committed to African American adult education. Its primary accomplishment was the publication of a series of materials related to cultural, social, and economic issues of the African American community. These became known as the Bronze Booklets. When AAAE funding support ended for the Harlem and Atlanta projects, the ANFE represented the next concrete project in African American adult education for the Corporation and the AAAE. We will return to the ANFE later. Let us first examine the AAAE's reaction to the first recommendation concerning promotional work in African American adult education. There are two points on which we will focus.

As will be recalled, the Carnegie Corporation's interest in African American adult education was mainly experimental. There was no commitment, other than exploratory, by Keppel or the AAAE to the Atlanta and Harlem adult education projects. Because the AAAE was dependent on the Corporation for its funding, the planned termination of funding to the projects despite the reports of success was not surprising. Nevertheless, Jones protested to Morse Cartwright the cessation of funding scheduled for the end of 1934.[32] Cartwright explained in a letter to Locke that Keppel "felt that the Negro adult education experiments were yet in such early stages that to propagandize for them at the present time might be dangerous."[33] What Keppel meant by "dangerous" is unclear. What does seem clear is that, despite the positive reports filed by Locke, Rose, and Hawes, Keppel considered African American adult education in its infancy and believed that efforts to implement a definite program of adult education were premature. This, of course, seems odd since the AAAE was only a few years older than the experiments. The net effect was to undermine Jones' and Locke's goal of having a person to promote adult education for the African American community. As noted earlier, Keppel may well have appreciated Locke's views on art and culture. But he saw the significance of the Harlem and Atlanta projects differently than either Jones or Locke did. Their commitment to these projects as African Americans was fundamentally different from that of Keppel or Cartwright. As African Americans, neither could be neutral or tentative in his judgment about these experiments. Wilson Record's commentary, noted at the beginning of this chapter, highlights this view. Keppel did not have the same level of understanding or commitment to African American adult education that Jones or Locke had despite his sympathetic view towards it.

Keppel did support the second recommendation made by

Locke in his evaluation report. The development of special materials related to African American adult education became the focal point of the ANFE. Organized by Jones, Locke, and Garnett Wilkinson, assistant superintendent of schools in Washington, D.C., the goals of the ANFE were:

1) The preparation and publication of study materials in Negro life and culture.
2) To publish syllabi outlines or booklets for the use of adult education groups concerning Negro life and culture.
3) To influence a constructive program and policy with respect to the extension of Adult Education work and opportunities among Negroes.[34]

THE BRONZE BOOKLETS

In fact, the ANFE devoted much of its attention to the preparation and publication of study materials for study groups in adult education. Jones became chairman of the organization, and Alain Locke served as editor of the series. Under Locke's editorship and with a grant from the Carnegie Corporation in the amount of $5250,[35] the ANFE published eight booklets.[36] The most noted of these was Ira Reid's *Adult Education Among Negroes* (1936). The other works included: Ralph Bunche, *World View of Race*; Alain Locke, *The Negro and His Music* and *Negro Art: Past and Present*; Sterling Brown, *The Negro in American Drama* and *The Negro in American Fiction and Poetry*; T. Arnold Hill, *The Negro and Economic Reconstruction*;[37] Eric Williams, *The Negro and the Caribbean*. Essentially, the ANFE set itself up as a publishing house for materials of African American adult education.

Yet, scarce financial resources and lack of a broad-based commitment to the ANFE led to its early demise. For example, financial records of the ANFE show that by 1940, four years after the publication of the first books in the series, the Carnegie Corporation's initial grant of $5250 still accounted for nearly eighty percent of the total revenue to the organization.[38] With individuals like John Hope, Mary McLeod Bethune, Charles S. Johnson,

Arthur Schomburg, and A. Philip Randolph, support for the organization might have been widespread.[39] However, the business of the organization was conducted essentially by two persons, Locke and Wilkinson; few of the other member attended meetings.[40]

Furthermore, in its largest single endeavor, the publication of the Bronze Booklets, control of editorial decisions rested not solely in the purview of the editor. Lyman Bryson, a professor at Columbia University, active in the AAAE, and also a member of the ANFE, represented the interests of the AAAE.[41] Locke deferred repeatedly to Bryson's judgment on whether certain of the manuscripts, principally those written by Bunche and Du Bois, were "passable."[42] Bryson was concerned about the radical perspective—Marxist in the case of Bunche and Marxist–Pan Africanist in the case of Du Bois. Bryson approved of Bunche's manuscript but did not approve Du Bois'. Du Bois' work was not published as part of the series.[43] Space does not permit detailed discussion of the correspondence between Du Bois and Locke, and Locke and Bryson on this subject. However, Bryson's influence is unmistakable.

Although requests from various groups for the materials came in regularly, the distribution of the materials was slow and painstaking and essentially fell to Locke to carry out. Moreover, the work of the ANFE was hampered by a lack of an effective plan or organization to facilitate the distribution and sale of the materials. It would appear that the initial enthusiasm and excitement for African American adult education sponsored by the AAAE and the Corporation had waned by 1940. As a result the organization, only one of several concrete manifestations of the AAAE's interest in African American adult education, had effectively ceased to operate only a few short years after its founding.[44]

SUMMARY

The Carnegie Corporation through the AAAE provided the support and encouragement of adult education programs throughout the country. The Corporation's primary purpose, however, was based on the idea of the diffusion of knowledge. What provided the impetus for adult education programs from the Corporation's viewpoint was the aim of making available to the general public adult educational opportunities that would enrich life and overcome the problems of a mass, industrial society. This view was carried out largely by Frederick Keppel as president of the Corporation.

The aims of the Corporation and of the AAAE became ever more clear when, despite positive reports, funding by the AAAE for each program was ended. Eugene Kinckle Jones, Alain Locke, and Mae C. Hawes, the principal African American figures in these projects, agreed with the aims for the projects and they were committed, as a result of their race, in a way that Cartwright and Keppel, for example, could not be. This difference in commitment led to disagreement and disappointment over the termination of the projects.

Nevertheless, needs identified in the evaluation of the projects by Locke and Jones led to the creation of the Associates in Negro Folk Education. This short-lived organization was dedicated to the preparation and publication of special materials related to African American adult education. It was responsible for the publication of the "Bronze Booklets," a series intended for use by groups discussing issues of concern to the African American community. However, a narrow base of support and financial dependency on the AAAE led to its demise. While the leaders of the ANFE perhaps did not see the organization as an independent entity, its existence did present an opportunity for the further development of African American adult education. Because those African Americans involved in the project were dependent on the AAAE and the Corporation for financial support, the development of a viable long-term program of adult education for African Americans did not materialize. Other priorities of the Corporation and the AAAE prevented the accomplishment of the goals envisioned by Jones, Locke, and others.

NOTES

1. Wilson Record, *Phylon*, v. 15, 3rd quarter, 1954. p. 231.
2. Andrew Hacker, *Two Nations: Separate, Hostile, and Unequal*. New York: Charles Scribner's and Sons, 1992. p. 34.
3. Malcolm Knowles, *A History of the Adult Education Movement in*

the United States. Huntington, N.Y.: Robert E. Krieger Publishing Company, 1977. p. 190. Reissued 1994 with new preface and bibliography, Malabar, FL: Krieger Publishing Company.

4. Harold W. Stubblefield, *Towards a History of Adult Education in America.* New York: Croom Helm, 1988. p. 24.

5. *Ibid.*, p. 29.

6. *Ibid.*, pp. 30–32.

7. Ellen C. Lagemann, *The Politics of Knowledge: The Carnegie Corporation, Philanthropy, and Public Policy.* Middletown, CT: Wesleyan University Press, 1989. p. 127.

8. Morse A. Cartwright, "Annual Report of the Director," in *Journal of Adult Education.* v. 3, 1931. p. 380.

9. For a fuller discussion of the motives of Keppel and the Corporation in African American education, see Ellen Lagemann, *The Politics of Knowledge*, pp. 127ff.

10. Cartwright, op. cit., p. 380.

11. Mae C. Hawes, "Racial Development and Cooperation," In *Journal of Adult Education,* v. 5, 1933. p. 301.

12. Morse A. Cartwright, op. cit., p. 352.

13. *Ibid.*

14. Ernestine Rose, "A Record of Two Experiments," In *Journal of Adult Education,* v. 5, 1933. p. 53.

15. *Ibid.*

16. *Ibid.*

17. Alain Locke, "The Harlem Experiment," in *Journal of Adult Education,* v. 5, 1933. p. 302.

18. John Brown Childs, *Leadership, Conflict, and Cooperation in Afro American Social Thought.* Philadelphia: Temple University Press, 1989. p. 95.

19. E. Rose, op. cit., p. 55.

20. *Ibid.*

21. *Ibid.*

22. Alain Locke, "Report on Negro Adult Education," dated March 15, 1934. Alain Locke papers, Writings by Locke folder. Moorland-Spingarn Research Center, Howard University, Washington, D.C.

23. Jeffrey Stewart, *The Biography of Alain Locke: Philosopher of the Harlem Renaissance, 1886–1930.* Unpublished doctoral dissertation: Yale University, 1979.

24. Lagemann, op. cit., p. 130.

25. Locke, "Report."

26. *Ibid.*

27. Locke agreed with Du Bois but did not completely reject Booker T. Washington's program for education. His views at the time are presented in "Negro Education Bids for Par." In the *Survey Graphic,* v. 54, 1925. pp. 567–570; and also in "Reciprocity Instead of Regimentation: Lessons of Negro Adult Education." In *Journal of Adult Education.* v. 6, 1934. pp. 418–420.

28. Locke, "Reciprocity Instead of Regimentation: Lessons of Negro Adult Education." In *Journal of Adult Education.* v. 6, 1934. p. 420.

29. Eugene Kinckle Jones, Letter to Morse A. Cartwright, dated April 2, 1934. Alain Locke papers, Correspondence folder. Moorland-Spingarn Research Center, Howard University, Washington, D.C.

30. Amy Rose, "Beyond Classroom Walls: The Carnegie Corporation and The Founding of the American Association for Adult Education." In *Adult Education Quarterly,* 1989. v. 39, no. 3. p.503.

31. Locke, "Final Memorandum: New Projects in Adult Education for Negroes." dated April 15, 1934. p. 1. Alain Locke papers. Writings by Locke file. Moorland-Spingarn Research Center, Howard University.

32. Jones, op. cit.

33. Morse A. Cartwright to Alain Locke, letter dated June 21, 1934. Alain Locke papers. Correspondence file. Moorland-Spingarn Research Center, Howard University.

34. Certificate of Incorporation of Associates in Negro Folk Education, April 7, 1936. Alain Locke papers. Organizations File. Moorland-Spingarn Research Center, Howard University, Washington, D.C.

35. Locke to Cartwright, Letter dated March 6, 1935. Alain Locke Papers. Correspondence file. Moorland-Spingarn Research Center, Howard University.

36. Eugene C. Holmes, "Alain Locke and the Adult Education Movement." In *Journal of Negro Education.* v. 14, 1965. p. 5.

37. T. Arnold Hill, president of the National Urban League, was asked to write on the subject of economic reconstruction after W. E. B. Du Bois' manuscript was rejected for publication.

38. "Associates in Negro Folk Education Financial Statement" dated May 21, 1940. Alain Locke Papers. Organizations file. Moorland-Spingarn Research Center, Howard University, Washington, D.C.

39. List of members, Associates in Negro Folk Education, dated February 4, 1935. Alain Locke Papers. Organizations file. Moorland-Spingarn Research Center, Howard University, Washington, D.C.

40. Associates in Negro Folk Education, resume of Annual Meeting, May 24, 1940. Alain Locke Papers. Organizations file. Moorland-Spingarn Research Center, Howard University, Washington, D.C.

41. Letter from Franklin Hopper to Morse A. Cartwright, dated January 22, 1935. Alain Locke Papers. Correspondence file. Moorland-Spingarn Research Center, Howard University, Washington, D.C.
42. Letter from Locke to Bryson dated June 8, 1936. Alain Locke Papers. Correspondence file. Moorland-Spingarn Research Center, Howard University, Washington, D.C.
43. The final version of the Du Bois manuscript is available in Herbert Aptheker, *Against Racism, Unpublished Essays, Papers, Addresses, 1887–1961*. Amherst: The University of Massachusetts Press, 1985. pp. 103–158.
44. Letter from Alain Locke to Mary Brady, dated November 25, 1945. Alain Locke Papers. Correspondence file. Moorland-Spingarn Research Center, Howard University, Washington, D.C.

REFERENCES

Aptheker, Herbert. 1985. *Against Racism, Unpublished Essays, Papers, Addresses, 1887–1961*. Amherst: The University of Massachusetts Press.

Associates in Negro Folk Education. 1936. "Certificate of Incorporation." dated April 7, 1936. Alain Locke Papers. Organizations File. Moorland-Spingarn Research Center, Howard University, Washington, D.C.

Associates in Negro Folk Education. 1935. "List of members." dated February 4, 1935. Alain Locke Papers. Organizations file. Moorland-Spingarn Research Center, Howard University, Washington, D.C.

Associates in Negro Folk Education. 1940. "Financial Statement." dated May 21, 1940. Alain Locke Papers. Organizations file. Moorland-Spingarn Research Center, Howard University, Washington, D.C.

Associates in Negro Folk Education. 1940. "Resume of Annual Meeting." dated May 24, 1940. Alain Locke Papers. Organizations file. Moorland-Spingarn Research Center, Howard University, Washington, D.C.

Cartwright, Morse A. 1931. "Annual Report of the Director." In *Journal of Adult Education*. v. 3, p. 380.

Cartwright, Morse A. 1932. "Report of the Director." In *Journal of Adult Education*, v. 4. p. 352.

Cartwright, Morse A. 1934. "Letter to Alain Locke." dated June 21, 1934. Alain Locke papers. Correspondence file. Moorland-Spingarn Research Center, Howard University.

Childs, John Brown. 1989. *Leadership, Conflict, and Cooperation in Afro American Social Thought.* Philadelphia: Temple University Press.

Hacker, Andrew. 1992. *Two Nations: Separate, Hostile, and Unequal.* New York: Charles Scribner's and Sons.

Hawes, Mae C. 1933. "Racial Development and Cooperation," In Journal of *Adult Education,* v. 5, pp. 301–303.

Holmes, Eugene C. 1965. "Alain L. Locke and Adult Education Movement." In *The Journal of Negro Education.* v. 34:1. pp. 5–10.

Hopper, Franklin. 1935. "Letter to Morse A. Cartwright." dated January 22, 1935. Alain Locke Papers. Correspondence file. Moorland-Spingarn Research Center, Howard University, Washington, D.C.

Jones, Eugene Kinckle. 1934. "Letter to Morse A. Cartwright." dated April 2, 1934. Alain Locke papers, Correspondence folder. Moorland-Spingarn Research Center, Howard University, Washington, D.C.

Knowles, Malcolm. 1977. *A History of the Adult Education Movement in the United States.* Huntington, N.Y.: Robert E. Krieger Publishing Company. Reissued 1994 with new preface and bibliography, Malabar, FL: Krieger Publishing Company.

Lagemann, Ellen C. 1989. *The Politics of Knowledge: The Carnegie Corporation, Philanthropy, and Public Policy,* Middletown, CT: Wesleyan University Press.

Locke, Alain. 1933. "The Harlem Experiment." in *Journal of Adult Education,* v. 5. pp. 301–303.

Locke, Alain. 1934. "Final Memorandum: New Projects in Adult Education for Negro Groups." dated April 15, 1934. Writings by Locke box. Moorland-Spingarn Research Center, Howard University, Washington, D.C.

Locke, Alain. 1934. "Report on Negro Adult Education," dated March 15, 1934. Alain Locke papers. Writings by Locke folder. Moorland-Spingarn Research Center, Howard University, Washington, D.C.

Locke, Alain. 1925. "Negro Education Bids for Par." In the *Survey Graphic,* v. 54. pp. 567–570.

Locke, Alain. 1934. "Reciprocity Instead of Regimentation: Lessons of Negro Adult Education." In *Journal of Adult Education.* v. 6, 1934. pp. 418–420.

Locke, Alain. 1934. "Final Memorandum: New Projects in Adult Education for Negroes." dated April 15, 1934. Alain Locke papers. Writings by Locke file. Moorland-Spingarn Research Center, Howard University.

Locke, Alain. 1935. "Letter to Morse A. Cartwright." dated March 6, 1935. Alain Locke Papers. Correspondence file. Moorland-Spingarn Research Center, Howard University.

Locke, Alain. 1936. "Letter from Locke to Bryson." dated June 8, 1936. Alain Locke Papers. Correspondence file. Moorland-Spingarn Research Center, Howard University, Washington, D.C.

Locke, Alain. 1945. "Letter from Alain Locke to Mary Brady." dated November 25, 1945. Alain Locke Papers. Correspondence file. Moorland-Spingarn Research Center, Howard University, Washington, D.C.

Record, Wilson. 1954. "Intellectuals in Social and Racial Movements." In *Phylon,* v. 15, 3rd quarter. pp. 231–242.

Rose, Amy. 1989. "Beyond Classroom Walls: The Carnegie Corporation and The Founding of the American Association for Adult Education." In *Adult Education Quarterly.* v. 39, no. 3. pp. 140–151.

Rose, Ernestine. 1933. "A Record of Two Experiments," In *Journal of Adult Education,* v. 5, p. 53–55.

Stewart, Jeffrey. 1979. *The Biography of Alain Locke: Philosopher of the Harlem Renaissance, 1886–1930.* Unpublished doctoral dissertation: Yale University.

Stubblefield, Harold W. 1988. *Towards a History of Adult Education in America.* New York: Croom Helm.

CHAPTER 6

SEPTIMA POINSETTE CLARK: UNSUNG HEROINE OF THE CIVIL RIGHTS MOVEMENT

OPAL V. EASTER

Septima Poinsette Clark was a black woman adult educator who fought for the civil and educational rights of her people. She was the director of education for the Highlander Folk School and the director of training of the Southern Christian Leadership Conference (SCLC). Little is known about her because, like many other women, her contributions were omitted from both black history and the adult education literature until recently. Wyatt Walker, former executive director of SCLC, called her, "one of the great spirits of the [civil rights] movement (and) one of the most unpublicized."[1]

Clark began teaching school in South Carolina in 1916, and spent the next 40 years teaching both children and adults. During this time she helped change the laws so that black teachers could teach in Charleston's public school system and receive equal pay.

In 1956, at the age of 58, she was terminated from her teaching position because she refused to give up her membership in the National Association for the Advancement of Colored People (NAACP). She then took a position as workshop director at the Highlander Folk School. Subsequently, she became the director of training. She helped lead workshops that trained both black and white civil rights and community leaders. These workshops led to the establishment of the Johns Island, South Carolina, Citizenship Schools which taught the people of the island reading, writing, and citizenship so that they could pass the test required to register to vote. The far-reaching goal of these schools was the democratic empowerment of the people. The Citizenship Schools, under Clark's direction, became the model for the voter registration drives of the Civil Rights Movement.

In 1961 Highlander, under threat of being closed by the State of Tennessee, transferred the Citizenship Schools to the Southern Christian Leadership Conference. Mrs. Clark transferred with the program and became SCLC's director of training. She was the first woman to be elected to SCLC's Board. Clark worked to establish citizenship schools throughout the South. Her efforts resulted in thousands of black people successfully passing the voter registration test, registering to vote, and standing up for their rights.

THE EARLY YEARS

Septima Poinsette was born in Charleston, South Carolina. Her father, Peter Poinsette, was born a slave who, she said, ". . . came out of slavery non-violent. He was a gentle, tolerant man who knew how to make the best of a situation." Her mother, Victoria Warren Poinsette, was born in Charleston but raised in Haiti. Septima describes her mother as a fiercely proud woman who was the disciplinarian of the family.[2]

There were four things Septima said she learned from her parents that helped her throughout her life. From her mother, she learned not to be afraid; from her father she learned to be truthful, strengthen people's weaknesses, and to see others as Christ sees them, recognizing that there is something fine and noble in everyone.[3]

Septima grew up in a time when the South was establishing segregation laws. Her elementary education was provided by the public elementary school for blacks (taught by white teachers) and a private school run by a black woman out of her home. Her high school years were spent at Burke Institute, the first high school for blacks in Charleston, and at Avery Normal Institute.[4] Avery, established in 1865, was one of the oldest and most influential private high schools in South Carolina. It was supported by the Congregational American Missionary Association to train black teachers.[5]

THE PROMISED LAND SCHOOL, JOHNS ISLAND, SOUTH CAROLINA

Septima, upon graduation from Avery at the age of 18, was able to secure a teaching position on Johns Island, one of the sea islands around the harbor of Charleston. South Carolina law allowed blacks to teach on the surrounding islands but not in Charleston. Johns Island had a population of about 2,700 very poor, mostly uneducated blacks who were descendants of cotton plantation African slaves. Remnants of the slave culture were evident in the language of the people, called Gullah. Gullah is composed of archaic English, standard English, and variations on English and African words. Most of the residents were farmers, and many had owned their own land since Reconstruction. These people were separated physically, socially, culturally, and psychologically from other blacks as well as whites since the island was not connected to the mainland for several hundred years.[6] Bridges were not built to the island until 1945.[7]

She describes the two-teacher, two-room school this way:

> . . . a schoolhouse constructed of boards running up and down with no slats in the cracks, and a fireplace at one end of the room that cooked the pupils immediately in front of it but allowed those in the rear to shiver and freeze on their uncomfortable, hard, back-breaking benches. . . .[8] It had shutters, but no window panes, no glass, no window sashes at all. Whenever the wind was blowing on one side, you had to keep those shutters closed. You opened the other side so you could have some light.[9]

Septima taught grades 5 through 8 and acted as the principal. Textbooks were scarce, and paper dry cleaning bags were used until blackboard and chalk finally arrived. "For reading we had to make up stories about things around them—the trees, the foliage, the animals. They learned to read those words first."[10] She and the other teacher earned a total of $60.00 per month for teaching 132 pupils. The one-room school for white children was across the road and had just a little more equipment than the black school. The white school had three students, and the white teacher was paid $85 per month.[11] These differences in facilities and wages were typical of the segregated schools in the South.

While on Johns Island, she taught adults as well as children.

I discovered that some of the men were beginning to get interested in a movement that was to mean much to the island folk. That was the organization of certain fraternal groups . . . Being members gave them standing among their fellow islanders . . . :in order to be functioning members of these lodges the men had to know the rituals, had to make speeches to their fellow members, even had to keep books. And to do these things it was almost necessary to be able to read and write. I say almost necessary because most of those men, being unable to read, had unusually good memories and were adept at memorizing. You could read something to a Johns Islander and he could repeat it to you. . . . But they still wanted to know how to read and write and do simple figuring. . . . So some of them began coming to the other Negro teacher and me for help. . . . We would . . . write out little speeches we had written for them, and they would memorize them; and they would make the speeches that we had helped them compose. . . . Pretty soon they wanted to . . . know how to read those speeches and even to write speeches of their own. . . . So they asked us if we wouldn't help them learn to read and write. . . . They would come to our boarding place after supper and we would try to teach them the rudiments of reading and writing. . . . The best thing about it was that they wanted to learn, that they were eager to improve themselves.[12]

Mrs. Clark wrote about the significance of her first experience on Johns Island in her biography, *Echo in My Soul*,

. . . It was helping these men . . . that I believe I . . . first became interested in a work that would command in later years so much of my time and zeal and enlist the help of many similarly interested. I'm speaking . . . of our efforts to combat adult illiteracy.[13]

She taught on Johns Island for three years and returned to Charleston after being offered a teaching position at Avery Normal Institute, her old ·high school. During this time she worked with the president of the National Association for the Advancement of Colored People (NAACP) to obtain signatures on petitions to persuade the legislature to allow black teachers to teach in the public schools for blacks. She went door-to-door and collected over ten thousand signatures. The law was passed in 1920, and in 1921 Charleston's black schools had black principals.

While in Charleston, Septima met and married Nerie Clark, a Navy sailor. They moved to North Carolina. They separated after the birth of their second child, and Mr. Clark died shortly thereafter. Mrs. Clark was now a single parent living with her in-laws. She taught in North Carolina for a year and then, leaving her son with his grandparents, returned to teaching on Johns Island. She moved to Columbia, South Carolina three years later.

In 1935 Miss Wil Lou Gray, the state supervisor for adult schools in Columbia, asked her to work in a program to teach inductees at Fort Jackson how to write their names so they could sign for their paychecks. (Mrs. Clark and other black teachers taught the black soldiers, and white teachers taught the white soldiers.) Using cardboard name cards developed by Miss Gray, Clark taught the soldiers to write their names, company numbers, and occupations by tracing—the kinesthetic method. Years later she shared this method with Bernice Robinson, the first Citizenship School teacher.[14]

While in Columbia she was active in the fight to win equal salaries for black teachers. She helped present the case to the NAACP attorney, Thurgood Marshall, who took the case to court. In 1945 the court ruled that black and white teachers with equal qualifications had to receive equal salaries.[15]

EDUCATIONAL PREPARATION FOR THE FUTURE

In addition to teaching in various towns in South Carolina, Mrs. Clark spent her summers in school learning techniques to make her a more effective teacher. In 1932 she attended Columbia University in New York taking classes in mathematics, astronomy, and curriculum development for slow learners. In 1937 she attended Atlanta University in Georgia, taking a class in working with people in rural areas and one on interpersonal relationships taught by W. E. B. Du Bois. She earned a bachelor's degree from Columbia in 1942 and went on to earn a master's degree from Hampton Institute.

PHILOSOPHY OF FREEDOM

Mrs. Clark believed in and taught responsible citizenship. She also believed that you must be willing to fight for your rights and not be afraid. She felt if the effort was put forth, change would eventually come. Her autobiography, *Echo in my Soul*, was ". . . dedicated to those unsung heroes who are endowed with the determination to work non-violently in the struggle for human dignity." She reminded all in the struggle that they must be prepared to suffer the harassments, reprisals, and intimidations that would come, without becoming bitter. She wrote, "These atrocities, fellow strugglers, will serve only as challenges to you [to] persistently . . . attack the inequities. . . ." She pointed out that the atrocities . . . "must be accepted as the price one pays in establishing freedom for all."[16]

PHILOSOPHY OF EDUCATION AND ITS ROLE IN FREEDOM FOR AFRICAN-AMERICAN PEOPLE

Mrs. Clark's philosophy of education and its role in freedom extended beyond the African American community. She said that by ". . . teaching the poor and underprivileged of my own underprivileged race . . ." she was able to help ". . . them raise themselves to a better status in life; I felt then that I would not only be serving them but serving my state and nation, too, all the people, affluent and poor, white and Black . . . I am more convinced than ever that in lifting the lowly we lift likewise the entire citizenship."[17]

In her 1975 annual Christmas message, she wrote,

The greatest evil in our country today is not racism but ignorance. I believe unconditionally in the ability of people to respond when they are told the truth. We need to be taught to study rather than to believe, to inquire rather than affirm.[18]

CLARK AND THE HIGHLANDER FOLK SCHOOL

In 1954 the Supreme Court of the United States ruled that racial segregation in public schools was unconstitutional. This case was argued and won by the NAACP. In 1955 South Carolina passed a law that said no city or state employee could belong to the NAACP (this was part of a systematic effort on the part of the southern states to eliminate NAACP activities in the area). Mrs. Clark was an active member of the NAACP, serving as the vice-president of the local chapter in Charleston.[19] She tried very hard to organize the teachers to fight the law but was unsuccessful because the teachers feared losing their jobs. The next school term her teaching contract was not renewed. It was not until 1976 that South Carolina admitted that she was unjustly terminated.

In 1956 Mrs. Clark joined Director Myles Horton and the staff at the Highlander Folk School in Monteagle, Tennessee as their director of summer workshops. She later became their director of education, responsible for all residential workshops for civil rights and community leaders, both black and white. She had spent the two previous summers at Highlander participating in workshops on school desegregation. Returning home, she encouraged others to attend the workshops and brought many people to Highlander. Esau Jenkins was one of these people.

Esau Jenkins met Mrs. Clark on Johns Island. He had come to

her at the age of 14 to learn to read. As an adult, he was a farmer and bus driver who had devoted himself to improving the quality of life for the people on the island. Mrs. Clark arranged for him to attend a week-long workshop at Highlander on scholarship. The workshop, ". . . like many other problem-centered Highlander workshops, dealt with pressing problems of local communities as well as with the problems and hopes of the world community."[20]

Mr. Jenkins' immediate problem was helping the people on the island to learn to read and write well enough to qualify as voters. He had been attempting to increase the number of black voters by teaching them the sections of the South Carolina Constitution that they needed to know to register to vote, while they rode on his bus. He was successful with some because they were able to memorize whole sections of the Constitution, but they still could not read. Mr. Jenkins asked Myles Horton to help him establish schools to teach people to read and write.[21] Jenkins provided the local leadership for these schools and Horton the funds.

Aimee Horton in her book on Highlander explains,

> The Johns Island program was undertaken as part of a three-year Community Leadership Training Project which Highlander had initiated in 1953 in one Alabama and several Tennessee rural communities. Supported by a grant from the Schwartzhaupt Foundation, its aim was "to train community leaders who will help bring about a better understanding of the nature of a democratic society." "The leaders," the proposal stated, "will be given guidance in increasing participation in local and national affairs, in stimulating interest in community problems, and in changing attitudes which limit democracy." . . . and, . . . "If properly trained and supervised, they should be able to develop other leaders from among their fellow citizens."[22]

THE CITIZENSHIP SCHOOLS

The Citizenship School on Johns Island did not come about overnight. It took approximately three years of planning, building community interest, overcoming fears, and training other leaders before the program began. During this period many others from the island, including the youth and young adults, came to Highlander through the efforts of Mrs. Clark and Mr. Jenkins. Horton and his wife also visited Johns Island to get to know the people and to let the people get to know them. Action plans resulting from visits to Highlander consisted of the establishment of a credit union, a health education program which eliminated deaths from diphtheria, home improvement projects, the reactivation of the Johns Island Civic Club, and the establishment of a cooperative store in which residents sold items to each other.

It was in this cooperative store that the Citizenship School began in 1957. While store activities took place in the front, the two rooms in the rear were used for the school. This way the school could be concealed from the white people who did not want blacks to learn to read, write, and most of all, vote. Classes took place for two hours, two nights a week for two months.[23]

Mrs. Clark found a teacher for the school. She was Bernice Robinson, who was a beautician and Mrs. Clark's cousin. She had attended several workshops at Highlander with Mrs. Clark. Robinson was paid $50.00 per month.[24] This was Highlander's policy even after other schools were established. Clark points out that teaching in the program was probably costing Robinson more than she was earning since she had to pay someone to watch her ill mother and was losing income from her business.

Robinson had no formal teacher training, but she was willing to try and promised to do what she could. The first class meeting she told her students, "I'm not really going to be your teacher. We're going to work together and teach each other."[25]

The curriculum was student-driven. In addition to learning to read, write their names, understand the State Constitution, and fill out the voter's registration card, the students were eager to learn how to complete money orders and how to order from a catalog. Olendorf describes Robinson's teaching methods:

Robinson developed a number of successful techniques. . . . She provided reading material relevant to their needs. She developed vocabulary and spelling lists from words they needed to know from the South Carolina Constitution and their everyday lives. . . . She asked them to tell stories about their work in the field and their homes. Then she put their stories on paper and told the students, "This is your story. We're going to learn how to read your story." Robinson knew this was a good way to teach, without ever having heard of the 'language experience' approach. Math was made relevant to them by using grocery ads and problems with practical applications: "How much do you expect to receive when you sell your crops."[26]

In addition, Clark ". . . devised a workbook that discussed such subjects as the South Carolina election laws, particularly those setting forth the requirements for registering and voting, the laws concerning social security, laws relating to taxes, . . . laws relating to the duties and functions of the school board; . . ." The information was rewritten in simple, easily comprehensible words. "My purpose, of course was not only to teach them how to read and write but to teach them at the same time things they would have to know in order to start on their way to becoming first-class citizens."[27] Clark and Robinson combined their techniques, resources, and information into a book for students called *My Citizenship Booklet*.[28]

The Citizenship School was so successful that others were established on Wadmalaw and Edisto Islands and in North Charleston. The same process of identifying community leaders and training them at Highlander also took place. In 1959–60, 182 people enrolled in citizenship schools on the three islands and in North Charleston; 65 registered to vote. In 1960–61, additional classes enrolled 111 black students; 105 registered to vote. Schools were also established on St. Helena and Daufuskie Islands. Robinson and Clark also organized classes in Huntsville, Alabama, and Savannah, Georgia.[29]

Robinson became the supervisor responsible for opening new classes; Mrs. Clark continued to raise funds for Highlander, recruit and train new teachers, and train community leaders. These teachers and community leaders came to Highlander, often at great personal risk, to learn how to make things better in their communities. These leaders, besides those who were chosen from the islands, included Rosa Parks, who shortly after returning from

Highlander, refused to give up her seat on a Montgomery, Alabama bus and sparked the Civil Rights Movement, and Fannie Lou Hamer, the founder of the Mississippi Democratic Freedom Party.

Mrs. Clark also trained some of the students who were involved in the sit-ins. In July, 1960 she wrote to Ella Baker, the executive director of the Southern Christian Leadership Conference, inviting her to help in the training. She wrote, "We are attempting to help these . . . young people . . . by bringing them to the school [Highlander] for a workshop on the tactics and techniques of follow-through in school desegregation, voter registration and leadership education. Won't you come to this workshop and show your experiences in the current problems." Baker went to Highlander and helped Clark train "young people for leadership roles in the civil rights movement."[30]

CLARK AND SOUTHERN CHRISTIAN LEADERSHIP CONFERENCE (SCLC)

In July, 1961, Highlander transferred the Citizenship Schools and the teacher training workshops to SCLC. Dr. Martin Luther King Jr. asked that Mrs. Clark transfer with the programs and become SCLC's director of education and training. Andrew Young, who was a Highlander staff person at the time, also transferred to SCLC. Bernice Robinson remained at Highlander.

SCLC's Dorchester Cooperative Community Center was established in McIntosh, Georgia. People were recruited and brought to the Center from all over the rural south by Mrs. Clark, Andrew Young, James Bevel, and his wife, Diane Nash Bevel.[31] Fairclough described the activity at the Center.

The week-long course gave poorly educated rural blacks a crash course in the American political system, including such down to earth advice as how to overcome the myriad (of) obstacles which tripped up would-be Black voters. Much of the course covered the "basics" of voter registration, how to locate the registrars, how to fill in the form, how to prepare for the literacy and "understanding" tests.[32]

It was hoped that course completers would be able to return to their homes, pass the voter's registration tests and start up classes in their communities. One of the people who attended the Center was Fannie Lou Hamer.

The schools spread quickly and "by September 1963, there were seven hundred teachers and fifty thousand new voters who could be traced to the Citizenship School movement."[33]

When not at the Center, Mrs. Clark

traveled throughout the Southern states directing workshops for SCLC. She instilled in the minds of her workshop participants that they must become cognizant of the non-partisan basis of the American System. They are taught their constitutional rights and how to organize to obtain the political power to get streetlights or better roads and schools in their part of town. The right to peaceful assembly and to petition for redress of grievances is related to how they can organize their own community for change.[34]

SUMMARY

Clark's work with Highlander, the Citizenship Schools, and the Southern Christian Leadership Conference were the significant high points of her professional career. In addition to her NAACP membership, she was an active member of the Alpha Kappa Alpha Sorority and served as Basileus for the Gamma Xi Omega Chapter in Charleston. In this leadership role, she initiated several health programs, including one to combat ringworm in black children. She was honored both by her local chapter and the national office of the sorority for fighting for human rights and for her contribution to desegregating the South.

She was a member of the board of the Community Chest of Charleston (approximately 1945) and worked with the Y.M.C.A., the Tuberculosis Association, and the Department of Health in

Charleston. In 1975 Mrs. Clark was elected to the same school board in Charleston that had not renewed her teaching contract. She was the first black woman elected to this school board. In 1978 she was given the Living the Legacy Award by President Carter in recognition of her work.[35]

Septima Clark died in 1987, her work done, but not completed. Those who live in the South Carolina low country still remember their teacher and leader. Many of the programs which she helped initiate are still in existence. There is a stretch of the interstate that runs through South Carolina that has been renamed the Septima P. Clark Memorial Highway as a monument to the woman who touched the lives of so many.

NOTES

1. Personal interview with Walker quoted in Adam Fairclough, *To Redeem the South of America: The Southern Christian Leadership Conference and Martin Luther King Jr.* (Georgia: University of Georgia Press, 1987), pp. 69–70.
2. Septima P. Clark, *Ready from Within: Septima Clark and the Civil Rights Movement*, ed. Cynthia Stokes Brown (California: Wild Tree Press, 1986), p. 88.
3. *Ibid.*, p. 98.
4. *Ibid.*, p. 101.
5. Asa H. Gordon, *Sketches of Negro Life and History in South Carolina*, 2nd ed., with foreword by Tom E. Terrill (South Carolina: University of South Carolina Press, 1971), p. 92.
6. Aimee I. Horton, *The Highlander Folk School: A History of Its Major Programs 1932–1961* (New York: Carlson Publishing, Inc., 1989), p. 215.
7. Clark, *Ready from Within*, p. 108.
8. Septima Clark, *Echo in My Soul* (New York: E.P. Dutton & Co., 1962) p. 38.
9. Clark, *Ready from Within*, p. 104.
10. *Ibid.*, p. 106.
11. *Ibid.*, p. 148.
12. Clark, *Echo in My Soul*, pp. 51–52.
13. *Ibid.*, p. 52.

14. *Ibid.*, p. 148.
15. Clark, *Ready from Within*, p. 148.
16. Clark, *Echo in My Soul*.
17. *Ibid.*, p. 52.
18. Felicia H. Felder, "Septima Poinsette Clark: She, Too, Helped Build America," *Negro History Bulletin* (Nov/Dec., 1978), p. 906.
19. *Ibid.* p. 906.
20. Horton, p. 216.
21. Sandra B. Oldendorf, "The South Carolina Sea Island Citizenship Schools, 1957–1961," *Women in the Civil Rights Movement* eds. Vicki Crawford, Jacqueline Anne Rouse, and Barbara Woods (New York: Carlson Publishing Inc. 1990), p. 171.
22. Horton, p. 217.
23. Clark, *Echo in My Soul*, p. 150.
24. *Ibid.* p. 150.
25. Personal interview with Ms. Robinson quoted in Oldendorf, p. 172.
26. Oldendorf, p. 172.
27. Clark, *Echo in My Soul*, p. 150.
28. Clark, *Ready from Within*, p. 51.
29. Oldendorf, p. 174; Horton, p. 225.
30. Grace Jordan McFadden, "Septima P. Clark and the Struggle for Human Rights," *Women in the Civil Rights Movement* eds. Vicki Crawford, Jacqueline Anne Rouse and Barbara Woods (New York: Carlson Publishing, Inc., 1990), p. 90.
31. Interview with Diane Nash Bevel after presentation on "Women in the Civil Rights Movement" at the Carter G. Woodson Regional Library in Chicago, Illinois, March 23, 1991.
32. Fairclough, pp. 69–70.
33. Oldendorf, p. 174.
34. McFadden, pp. 90–91.
35. Gerda Lerner, *The Majority Finds Its Past: Placing Women in History*, (New York: Oxford University Press, 1979), p. 110.; Felder, p. 906; McFadden, p. 65.

CHAPTER 7

AFRICAN AMERICAN LEADERSHIP, RELIGIOUS EXPRESSION, AND INTELLECTUAL DISCOURSE: UNCOVERING MALCOLM X's LEGACY TO ADULT EDUCATION

ANDREW P. SMALLWOOD

We must establish all over the country schools of our own to teach our own children to become scientists, to become mathematicians. We must realize the need for adult education and job retraining programs that will emphasize a changing society in which automation will play a key role. We intend to use tools of education to help raise our people to an unprecedented level of excellence and self-respect through their own efforts. (Malcolm X - June 28, 1964).[1]

INTRODUCTION

Over the course of many centuries Africans have attempted to assert their humanity, often facing inhumane circumstances manifest in the social conditions of slavery and racial segregation. African Americans throughout the United States have looked to the importance of leaders whose commitment and sincerity to the struggle for inclusion and self-determination would shine a light of hope in a world often ravaged with various socioeconomic problems. It is in this context that a few black leaders expressed the anguish of their constituents with both a critical and constructive public discourse to combat the racial stereotypes and discuss the positive contributions of Africa and African people to world civilization. It is in this tradition that Malcolm X (El-Hajj Malik El Shabazz) rose from the depths of despair to become an international figure. This chapter examines the oft overlooked aspect of adult education of Malcolm X a major figure in the early twentieth century. In the role of Muslim minister and Civil Rights leader, Malcolm X engaged in an intellectual public discourse that represented a pedagogical approach to adult learning. A. Peter Bailey, a former assistant of Malcolm X's, stated, "Malcolm was a Master Teacher" whose loss to the black community is significant, because few individuals carry this special title and responsibility, and have the ability to espouse a rhetoric of black liberation.[2] I propose that Malcolm X can be referred to as an Intellectual Aesthetic who through his leadership expressing his thoughts and ideas, advanced the concept of adult education for African Americans. To explore this idea further I provide an overview of the function of religious expression for African Americans, examine the origins of the Nation of Islam (NOI), and the function of adult education in the organization to examine Malcolm X's early ministry and locate his role as an adult educator.

BLACK CULTURE AND ADULT EDUCATION IN THE EARLY TWENTIETH CENTURY

The call for African American adults to be educated about their history, according to the late black historian John Henrik Clarke, goes back to the beginning of the twentieth century when scholars such as W. E. B. Du Bois and Carter G. Woodson took the position that the contributions of Africans in the diaspora were both important and worthy of further study.[3] Alain Locke, a proponent of African American adult education during the early twentieth century, expressed the importance for African Americans to understand their history and contributions to world civilization:

The study of racial and group history of group contributions to culture, or even of specific group problems, is sound and constructively educative. In fact, these emphases have been found to be magnets of interest and galvanizers of the adult education program groups . . . Social education is an unavoidable aspect of adult education, and an inescapable obligation of adult educators.[4]

It becomes clear that Locke's position on the development of educational programs for African Americans should reflect their cultural experiences and needs in order to be successful (see Guy and Gyant chapters).

Both Woodson and Locke were early twentieth-century advocates for educating African American adults. As scholar-activists, they maintained an intense desire to fight against the notions that black people made no significant contributions to American history. In his book, *Mis-education of the Negro* (1933), Woodson's criticism of education, particularly during the Civil War, points to the emphasis on Europe in teaching world history while the contributions of Africans were negated.

In history of course, the Negro had no place in this curriculum. He was pictured as a human being of lower order, unable to subject passion to reason, and therefore useful only when made the hewer of wood and the drawer of water for others.[5]

As an advocate for educating African American adults, Woodson believed in a form of education that would do more than just promote knowledge for knowledge's sake:

Real education means to inspire people to live more abundantly, to learn to begin with life as (people) find it and make it better, but the instruction so far given to Negroes in college and universities has worked to the contrary.[6]

Woodson's statement addresses the deficiency of formal education for addressing the needs and concerns of African American adults at that time. Additionally, he is calling for research that is culturally and socially relevant to black life. It is the ongoing concern of misrepresenting African American contributions to American history via miseducation in public schools that would be later addressed vigorously at the height of the Civil Rights era. Here the Nation of

Islam (NOI), led by Elijah Muhammad and Malcolm X, carried the gauntlet laid down by Locke, Woodson, Garvey, Du Bois, and others in advocating a reeducation of black people, recognizing their historical accomplishments and contributions while emphasizing the experiences of African Americans rooted in their own culture and traditions.

From his time in prison until his death, Malcolm X continually studied the historical and social problems of African American people. Examination of his personal research in existing speeches, lectures, interviews, and organizational meetings, Malcolm shows what falls within the intellectual tradition of scholar-activist, which entails educating black people about their contributions to world civilization.

THE IMPORTANCE OF THE RELIGIOUS EXPRESSION FOR AFRICAN AMERICANS

The role of organized religion in most societies is important for a group of people to understand their collective mission in relation to a supreme force. The people in the society are provided with both direction and purpose to act in the most correct way.

To understand religion for African Americans we must examine the context of social events which shape their religious expression. Noted black studies scholar Maulana Karenga cites research documenting highly evolved black religious expression in ancient African civilizations such as Egypt and Mali, at least two thousand years before the birth of Christ.[7] This demonstrates the long tradition of black religious expression prior to European enslavement of Africans in the sixteenth century. During the period when millions of Africans were forcibly placed into slavery by various European countries, their religious expression changed substantially. Africans were made to convert to Christianity; therefore, religion became a mechanism for white social control of black people. In many instances both free and enslaved blacks adapted their Christian teachings to address survival during slavery and segregation in the United States.

During this period there were few opportunities for black people to receive education. Reading and writing were viewed by many slave owners as a threat to the institution of slavery, as it was feared that black slaves would understand their potential in society and run away.

To circumvent laws in the southern United States prohibiting blacks from being legally educated, the black church played a vital role educating free and enslaved black people. In examining literature on the historical role of the black church for African Americans, Karenga states:

> The Black church has been important as (1) "a spiritual sanctuary" during enslavement, (2) an important "agency of social reorientation and reconstruction" of values, (3) a "center for economic cooperation" to bring community resources together for shared growth and educational projects, (4) a way of "setting up schools and training ministers and teachers and raising funds to carry out these projects," and (5) a way to support "social change and struggle, providing leaders and leadership at various points in the struggle for Black liberation and a truly higher level of human life."[8] Points four and five help serve as an important context for examining Malcolm X as a religious figure.

Education in the African American church has served, first, as a training ground for black ministers, and second, as a way to teach religious doctrine of various faiths. For black people forcibly converted to Christianity, this has meant a predominantly Christian form of worship and thus a religious education focusing on the Judeo-Christian traditions brought to the United States from Europe.

An important role of black churches has been the provision of resources to black people when segregation was widely accepted and education for blacks was generally inferior to whites. The most valuable resources provided were in the form of the development of black leadership. Black religious leaders organized and mobilized black community support and provided moral leadership and political influence historically for African Americans.

THE HISTORY OF THE NATION OF ISLAM AND THE FUNCTION OF EDUCATION

Segregation started growing in the 1870's after the end of southern Reconstruction in the United States, when an increase of violence against black people resulted in lynchings through the 1930's Additionally, an increase in riots resulted in numerous black deaths throughout the early twentieth century. These adverse conditions gave rise to the political leadership of Marcus Garvey and his UNIA organization whose call for black pride and racial unity resonated among many Africans Americans in the early twentieth century. Adversity also gave rise to a new voice of religious leadership and ideology for some African Americans (see Colin chapter). The twentieth century Muslim movement is linked to Noble Drew Ali's founding of the Moorish Science Temple in Newark, New Jersy, in 1913.[9] After Ali's death, several factions of the organization developed and were based in Chicago, Illinois. With the influence of the Marcus Garvey Movement, the Moorish Science Temple and the Harlem Renaissance of the 1920's and early 1930's, the Nation of Islam was founded in Detroit, Michigan, during the summer of 1930.[10]

The organization's founder, W. D. Fard (aka Fard Muhammad), was a man of unknown mixed racial heritage acknowledged by followers to be of Arabic ethnicity. As a textile salesperson, Fard Muhammad was able to talk to people about Islam and then he began teaching about foreign countries, physical health, and diet. He then proclaimed that the true religion for black people was not Christianity but Islam. Muhammad used the Bible and the Koran to teach black people about "their" religion.[11]

Fard's ideology combined various writings of the time including literature, anthropology, Christianity, and Freemasonry. After meeting in the homes of his followers and then securing space for a temple of worship, Fard Muhammad began to criticize whites for the deplorable conditions blacks experienced. Fard personally taught temple members who were illiterate how to read and gave historical knowledge to inspire them. Fard's teachings were identified as symbolic and thus required his personal interpretation. His writings consisted of two works, *The Secret Ritual of the Nation of Islam*, transmitted orally, and *Teaching for the Lost Found Nation of Islam in a Mathematical Way*, given to registered members. Fard Muhammad personally instructed each of his assistants to carry on his message after he left the organization due to a hostile political climate from rival groups and police harassment.[12]

One of Fard's assistants was Elijah Poole (later Elijah Muhammad) who, after hearing Fard's message, became mesmerized and joined the organization under Fard Muhammad's leadership. After Fard's departure, Elijah Muhammad became the principal leader of the NOI in 1934 and, according to him, was instructed by Fard to continue his teachings. According to his biographer Claude A. Clegg, Elijah Muhammad as leader of the organization for forty years, made no significant changes in the ideology of the organization from the time of Fard Muhammad.[13]

In examining the development of Malcolm X's adult education ideology, it is important to understand the influence of the NOI on him. After having been introduced to the NOI by his family while in prison, Malcolm eventually accepted the teachings of Elijah Muhammad. Upon his release from prison, Malcolm moved back to Michigan where he was raised to become an active participant in the organization. What made the NOI attractive to Malcolm X and other African Americans is its teaching about racial pride and blacks' historical accomplishments, while offering criticisms of problems resulting from racism. Elijah Muhammad and his ministers taught black people about their positive historical contributions to the development of civilization. Part of this message was based on the "racial superiority" of blacks over whites and divine retribution of whites for black suffering.[14]

In the NOI, history is combined with mythology and promotes the understanding of the black contributions to the origins of civilization. Thus, an alternative view of history is used to explain white domination and black suffering.[15]

In addition to hearing the teachings of NOI doctrine through Fard, Elijah and other ministers, new members were required to demonstrate their knowledge and commitment of these teachings through a number of steps before they were admitted into the organization.

To officially join the movement, the interested observer had to first write out a letter stating that he or she had accepted the teachings of the Muslims and would like to be given an original name. If the letter contained grammatical or spelling errors, it would be returned to the applicant for rewriting. After an acceptable correspondence was submitted, the new convert would have to memorize and learn, to the satisfaction of the leadership, a number of lessons that dealt with the philosophy of the Nation. The first lesson, "Student Enrollment," is a list of ten questions and answers about various population groups, the size of the earth, and the "Original Man." The next lesson, "Actual Facts," consists of eighteen statements on the natural features of the earth (such as mountains, oceans, and deserts) and their measure-ments. "English Lesson No. C1," part three, is a series of thirty-six questions and answers that focus on Fard's mission and the predicament of African-Americans. The last teachings, "Lost Found Moslem Lesson No. 1 and 2," are a battery of fifty-four queries and solutions that concentrate on geographic statistics as well as the history of black people, the "white devils," and the end of the white world. Taken together, the lessons were taught in classes attended by initiates fed up with their plight in America.[16]

In order to carry out the teachings of the organization and maintain control and discipline, three separate groups existed within the Nation of Islam. The Fruit of Islam (FOI), was the paramilitary wing of the organization, teaching "manhood" to its male members. The Muslim Girls Training - General Civilization Class (MGT-GCC) taught the women about womanhood and culture, and the University of Islam taught the children. Traditional gender roles for men and women were stressed and socializing outside of the NOI membership was highly discouraged.[17] The Fruit of Islam was a group established by male members of the organization responsible for enforcing laws within the temple, responsible for disciplining its members, and teaching men how to behave under the rules of the organization. The MGT-GCC as the counterpart to the FOI taught women their role in both domestic and temple life. Finally, the University of Islam was engaged in primary and some secondary instruction on mathematics, astronomy, and world civilization for children.[18]

The type of adult education in the first two groups conducted was in support of preserving the organization's ideology through the socialization of its members rather than fostering critical and analytical thinking.

From the beginning, the new convert's role in temple life was determined by a structured arrangement of authority and obligations. As much as possible, the Nation isolated the individual Muslim from those outside influences it deemed destructive and attempted to redefine the values of followers within the context of Fardian Islam. To do this, the leadership of the temple waged a propaganda war against white America to the extent that it was clear to all who entered the temple that they were surely in another world. Nothing in Western society was sacred or revered, and the symbols of the white world were singled out for scorn.[19]

Thus, the religious teachings were left to Elijah Muhammad and organizational ministers such as Malcolm X.

The curriculum of NOI schools reflects the organization's social values. The curriculum in the schools was divided into two types; *Intensive*—regarding specified knowledge based on subject matter and *Extensive*—group cultural norms. The FOI and MGT-GCC engage in extensive education.[20] Barbara Whiteside also observes:

These classes [were] held to impart knowledge and to disseminate information that is important to the Muslim lifestyle. . . . The divine nature of the Black Man and his glorious past seems to be the doctrine held in the highest esteem by the [NOI].[21]

Here we see an organization teaching people the importance of knowing their collective heritage in order to understand their "true" place in the world aside from racist and segregationist practice of society. With his conversion, Malcolm X joined the NOI using his historical knowledge, organizational doctrine and pedagogy to convert and transform its members. When examining the history of the NOI and other variables defining culture, we must examine Malcolm X's own unique voice within the context of the organization. It is from this point we can understand his relationship to the organization as a leader and educator.

THE EMERGING MINISTRY OF MALCOLM X

When examining research discussing Malcolm X, the issue of religion is often overlooked in his intellectual-humanistic development. Scholars who do address the evolution of his religious ideology do so in the context of his Christian upbringing, his conversion to the NOI, and his acceptance of a more orthodox form of Islam. Religious doctrine was important in providing a base for Malcolm X to interpret and discuss social issues regarding the African American experience. Theological training provided a foundation for Malcolm to examine world events (secular) in the context of the Biblical and Koran (sacred) text. In the NOI, Malcolm was personally trained by Elijah Muhammad just as Muhammad was trained by NOI founder Fard Muhammad. Then Malcolm X was able to disseminate the information through his public lectures and sermons infusing history, culture, and politics into a social analysis.

To understand the evolution of Malcolm X's religious beliefs, we must examine him in the context of the African American religious tradition. Malcolm X's father, Earl, served as a Baptist preacher and was a strong presence in the Little home. His untimely death led to the subsequent demise of the family with Louise Little (Malcolm's mother) suffering a nervous breakdown, becoming institutionalized, and her children being sent to different foster homes. Having grown up in the tradition of the black church, Malcolm X witnessed his father, a black preacher, infuse Biblical text and social problems facing blacks into a powerful message. Though his father was a Baptist minister, Malcolm eventually rejected Christianity and organized religion until he joined the NOI while in prison in the 1940's. The death of his father, the institutionalization of his mother resulting in the break-up of his family all contributed to his rejection of Christianity and organized religion altogether. Malcolm X's hatred toward religious people may also have been due to the domineering influence of his white foster parents and the resentment of being forced to attend church.[22] From this time until his incarceration, Malcolm X developed a hatred toward religion and he eventually became an atheist.[23]

As a young adult, Malcolm X struggled to earn a living working odd jobs such as shoeshine boy, railroad porter, and restaurant waiter, among other things. Eventually, he became frustrated and lived the life of a hustler, numbers runner, reefer peddler, and burglar.

It is the limited opportunity for economic advancement that attracted the most despondent African Americans (ex-convicts, drug addicts, pimps, and prostitutes ignored by the black Christian church) to Elijah Muhammad's message of nation building. Having been influenced by nationalist teachings of the Marcus Garvey Movement, the NOI emphasized economic independence from white society for its members through support of organizational businesses. Muhammad sought the poorest and most downtrodden black people to join the NOI. Richard B. Turner notes:

> While he was in prison in Michigan, [in the 1940's] Muhammad saw that black religious and political organizations had not developed programs to rehabilitate the lowest of the black lower class—the pimps, prostitutes, drug addicts, and young criminals like Detroit Red. After World War II, he changed the agenda of the Nation of Islam to concentrate on this group. He believed that knowledge of black peoples' true history and identity could transform this group into useful members of the black community.[24]

After being introduced to the teachings of Elijah Muhammad and the NOI by his siblings, Malcolm returned to a religious message rooted in cultural pride focusing on current problems facing black people in their communities. As part of the their theological teachings, the NOI emphasizes black racial pride. While in the NOI, Malcolm X used the religious ideology of Elijah Muhammad to emphasize the importance of black history and racial pride.

Malcolm X, a prodigious worker, first started in the Detroit temple to spread the religious message of Elijah Muhammad and he quickly became the Assistant Minister.[25] As he was given more responsibility and authority, he then was sent to other cities to start temples and increase the membership and financial support base for the fledgling organization.[26] Malcolm later was put in charge of developing the organization's newspaper which became the successful "Muhammad Speaks" organ and provided weekly articles for members and served as means for disseminating Elijah Muhammad's message to black adults.[27]

An attractive aspect of the NOI for disenfranchised blacks was that the organization served as an alternative critical voice of both the government and black organizations (Christian churches and later Civil Rights organizations in the 1950's) that either failed to assist them or pushed for an integrationist agenda for African American people. With strong critical public rhetoric, a focus on incarcerated black males and poor black people, and various businesses including their own newspaper, the NOI established a niche in the African American community which ensured its growth in membership.

Under the leadership of Elijah Muhammad, the NOI was interested in promoting social purity for members of its organization, thus requiring new members to give up alcoholic beverages, dancing, swearing, and other social activities.

It is important to note that Malcolm X's intellectual development and use of history pre-dates his joining the Nation of Islam. As result of his intense study and intellectual discourse while in prison, Malcolm was able to become versed in scholarly books in the social and behavioral sciences. This suggests that the historical knowledge he received was a result of his self-directed learning in addition to his religious teachings in the Nation of Islam.

As a member of the NOI, Malcolm accepted the philosophy of the organization's leader, Elijah Muhammad, whose adaptation of Islam had elements of Garvey's Black Nationalism. Emphasis on African American cultural celebration through social separation were common Black Nationalist themes shared by both organizations.[28] The influence on Malcolm X becomes clear when examining his speeches and writings stressing knowledge of African American history and culture.

Upon his departure from the NOI, Malcolm went further and openly accepted Black Nationalism; his political organization, The Organization of Afro-American Unity (OAAU), advancing political empowerment and Pan-Africanism, sought to develop linkages between African Americans with continental Africans to address problems resulting from European cultural hegemony.[29]

MALCOLM X: AN EDUCATOR OF BLACK ADULTS

When examining Malcolm X's experiences as an adult educator, Coomb's definition of nonformal education as cited by Ewert is appropriate for this essay. "Any organized educational activity outside the established formal system . . . that is intended to serve identifiable learning clienteles and learning objectives."[30]

When we examine Malcolm X's life, there is a significant

difference between him and other black leadership figures of the twentieth century: his educational background. Meier and Franklin state in their book, *Black Leaders of the 20th Century*, that in many instances these individuals received a high-school if not college education. Malcolm X's highest level of formal educational attainment was eighth grade. Thus, the nonformal educational attainment Malcolm X gained through his life experiences would eventually prepare him for his role as a black leader.

The genesis of Malcolm X as a community educator occurred during his incarceration in prison in the late 1940's. Here Malcolm rediscovered his passion for learning and focused on history and philosophy to understand the larger world outside his jail cell. Malcolm X's use of historical knowledge helped him in prison to become a successful debater.[31]

The subject of history is one that had a significant impact on the education of Malcolm X while in prison. During his time in prison, Malcolm was essentially removed from society and forced to reexamine the direction in which his life was headed. With the encouragement of fellow prisoner "Bimbi," Malcolm X discovered the power of learning through reading books about history and leading historical figures such as Frederick Douglass, Marcus Garvey, Ghandi, and Nat Turner. He discussed in his autobiography an intense desire for learning that pushed him to read and copy every word in the dictionary so as to get the full meaning of the books he was reading.[32] This desire for learning had Malcolm reading at night using minimal light and eventually impairing his eyesight. While in prison Malcolm also participated in prison debates, competing with other prison and college debate teams, sharpening his intellectual and analytical skills in a public forum.[33]

After he joined the NOI, Malcolm X served as an advocate for the public recognition of African American history which is part of the NOI's ideology. Malcolm's study of history helped him to better understand the plight of black people and later to communicate this understanding to them. Malcolm's use of historical information in his public discourse in black communities allowed him to educate black people about the root of the problems in their communities.

When examining Malcolm X as a member of the NOI, we see how he frequently connected historical events to current social problems facing black people. In William Sales's interview with Benjamin

Karim, Malcolm's former assistant minister, Karim recalls Malcolm teaching leadership classes:

> Malcolm X ran the Public Speaking class for brothers who wanted to be ministers. The curriculum was ancient history broken down into the Hittites, the Egyptians, the Assyrians, Babylonians all the way up through the Persians and Rome, the Crusades and the Moors in Spain. We had to read every newspaper, the N.Y. Times, the U.S. News and World Report, the Chinese Peking Review, London Times. Every week we had to keep abreast and see historically how everything came to this point, the history of slavery. . . . This was the class that he set up. There is no college class, calculus, trigonometry that was as rough as that Public Speaking class.[34]

Malcolm used this emphasis on history to teach black adults and help build the organization in the process.

Malcolm X continued to discuss current problems resulting from the historical conditions of racism facing African American people in the United States. Many writers reflect on the importance of Malcolm X's public discourse on various aspects of history, his personal history, African American history and U.S. history, as a pedagogical approach in teaching/preaching the doctrine of Elijah Muhammad and his organization. Malcolm X's belief in the importance of historical knowledge for African American people is mentioned even after his separation from the organization. While in the NOI, Malcolm used the organization's ideology as a foundation for reaching disenfranchised black people and criticized society's role in creating black ghettos.

In the period after Malcolm's departure from the NOI, he was left to develop both a philosophy and strategy to build his religious organization, the Muslim Mosque Incorporated (MMI), and his political organization, the Organization of Afro-American Unity (OAAU). By publicly identifying with Black Nationalist philosophy, Malcolm X continued to emphasize use of cultural history as a strategy for African American empowerment.[35]

As a religious organization, the NOI was successful in reaching many disenfranchised blacks and offering them hope for a better future. With the NOI's emphasis on black racial superiority and divine retribution for White supremacy, the organization provided an alternative voice of hope for blacks frustrated by racism in society and ignored by the traditional black Christian church, which often ignored segregation and lynchings of black men.

With his religious conversion and admittance into the NOI, we find Malcolm X had a clear purpose and direction for his individual talents. By serving the organizational leader Elijah Muhammad, Malcolm's focus was on spreading Elijah Muhammad's word to black people. Having been saved from a life of despair by the NOI, Malcolm quickly put forth all of his energy into building the organization so that more people could benefit from hearing the message of Elijah Muhammad and his representatives. When we examine Malcolm X's role in the NOI we see him being the beneficiary of education that is part of the organization's religious canon.

In his ministerial role, through his proselytizing, Malcolm X continued in the tradition of the African American clergy as community educators. With the growth of the NOI, and Malcolm's rise to national leadership, his status as a master teacher spreading the message of Elijah Muhammad took on a national significance. Malcolm's travels across the United States organizing new "temples" and would lead him to becoming more visible as a minister spreading the NOI doctrine.[36] In addition to reaching African Americans in their communities, he also attracted black people across economic classes in the United States as well.

CONCLUSION

Since the time of his death, the unique contributions of Malcolm X have been examined and reassessed with additional insight from former colleagues, friends and relatives. The scope and universality of Malcolm's message is considerable given the recognition of Malcolm X internationally and with ideologically diverse members of the African American community claiming him as their hero (rapper/activist Chuck D and Supreme Court Justice Clarence Thomas among others). The statement at the beginning of this article was made by Malcolm X at a Harlem, New York, rally to announce the formation of his second new organization, The Organization of Afro-American Unity, which he publicly discusses a program of action that underscores in part the importance of adult education in both society and for his new organization as an approach to address problems in black communities. What is evident in viewing the totality of Malcolm X's leadership is that his posture is indicative of a pedagogical thrust clearly locating him in the tradition of black adult educators whose discourse transcended the social malaise of racism to inspire their constituents to shed their acceptance of social and psychological inferiority and move toward black empowerment through cultural celebration and collective action.

REFERENCES

Ani, Marimba. *Yurugu: An African-Centered Critique of European Cultural Thought and Behavior*. Trenton, NJ: Africa World Press, 1994.

Asante, Molefi K. *Kemet, Afrocentricity, and Knowledge*. Trenton, NJ: Africa World Press, 1990.

Franklin, John H. and Alfred Moss. *From Slavery to Freedom*. 7th ed. New York: McGraw-Hill, 1994.

Haley, Alex. *Alex Haley Papers*. Schomburg Center for Research in Black Culture, The New York Public Library.

Malcolm X. *The End of White World Supremacy: Four Speeches by Malcolm X*. ed. Benjamin Karim. New York: Merlin House, 1971.

_____. *Malcolm X: The Last Speeches*. ed. Bruce Perry. New York: Pathfinder Press, 1989.

_____. *Malcolm X: Make It Plain*. Produced and Directed by Orlando Bagwell. 150 min. A Blackside Inc./Rojo Production Film, 1994, videocassette.

Mealy, Rosemari. *Fidel & Malcolm X: Memories of a Meeting*. Melbourne, Australia: Ocean Press, 1992.

Stewart, James B. "Reaching for Higher Ground: Toward an Understanding of Black/Africana Studies" in *Africana Studies: A Disciplinary Quest for Both Theory and Method*. Jefferson, NC: McFarland, 1997 and The Afrocentric Scholar. Vol. 1, No. 1. 1992.

Turner, Richard B. *Islam in the African American Experience*. Bloomington, IN.: Indiana University Press, 1997.

West, Cynthia S. "Nation Builders: Female Activism in The Nation of Islam, 1960-1970." Ph.D. Dissertation, Temple University, 1994.

NOTES

1. Malcolm X, *By Any Means Necessary*, George Breitman, ed. (2nd ed. New York: Pathfinder Press, 1992), 45.
2. Malcolm X, *Malcolm X: Make It Plain*, Produced and Directed by Orlando Bagwell,150 min., A Blackside Inc./Rojo Prod. film, 1994, videocassette.
3. John Henrik Clarke, "Africana Studies: A Decade of Change, Challenge and Conflict," in *The Next Decade: Theoretical and Research Issues in Africana Studies*, James Turner, ed. (Ithaca, NY: Africana Studies and Research Center, 1984), 31.
4. Alain Locke, *Negro in America* (Chicago: The American Library Association, 1933), 89.
5. Carter G. Woodson, *The Mis-education of the Negro*, (1933; reprint, New York: AMS Press, 1972), 21.
6. Ibid., 29.
7. Maulana Karenga, *Introduction to Black Studies*, (2nd ed. Los Angeles: University of Sankore Press, 1994), 212-230.
8. Ibid., 234.
9. Clifton E. Marsh, *Black Muslims to Muslims: The Resurrection Transformation, and Change of the Lost-Found Nation of Islam in America*, (Lanham, MD: Scarecrow Press, 1996), 29.
10. Claude A. Clegg, *An Original Man*, (New York: St. Martin's Press, 1997), 20; Marsh, *From Black Muslims to Muslims*, 37.
11. C. Eric Lincoln, *The Black Muslims in America*, (Boston: Beacon Press, 1961; reprint, Trenton, NJ, Africa World Press, 1994), 11-12.
12. Ibid., 14-15.
13. Clegg, *An Original Man*, 105.
14. Ibid., 21.
15. Ernest Allen, Jr., "Religious Heterodoxy and Nationalist Tradition: The Continuing Evolution of the Nation of Islam" in *The Black Scholar*, 26, 2-4, (Fall-Winter 1996), 10-11.
16. Clegg, *An Original Man*, 26-27.
17. Ibid., 100-101.

18. Michael E. Dyson, *Making Malcolm: The Myth and Meaning of Malcolm X*, 148.

19. Clegg, *An Original Man*, 28.

20. Barbara J. Whiteside, *A Study of the Structure, Norms and Folkways of the Educational Institutions of the Nation of Islam in the United States from 1932 to 1975*. (Ed.D. Diss., Wayne State University, 1987), 43.

21. Ibid., 41-42, 46.

22. Bruce Perry, *Malcolm: The Life of a Man who Changed Black America*, (Barrytown, NY: Station Hill Press, 1991), 32.

23. Malcolm X, *The Autobiography*, (as told to Alex Haley) 1965. (Reprint, New York: Ballantine, 1988), 153.

24. Richard B. Turner, *Islam in The African American Experience*, (Bloomington, IN.: Indiana University Press, 1997), 182.

25. Perry, *Malcolm*, 146.

26. Ibid., 146-147.

27. Clegg, *An Original Man*, 116.

28. Clegg, *An Original Man*, 41-73; Essien-Udom, *Black Nationalism: A Search for an Identity in America*, 7, 257-258, 269-270; Malcolm X, *The Autobiography*, 162.

29. Malcolm X, *Malcolm X Speaks*, ed. George Breitman (New York: Grove Press, 1965), 21-22.

30. Merrill D. Ewert, "Adult Education and International Development" in *The Handbook of Adult Education*, Phyllis M. Cunningham and Sharan B. Merriam eds., (San Francisco: Jossey-Bass, 1990), 84.

31. Malcolm X, *The Autobiography*, 154, 157, 158.

32. Ibid., 172-173.

33. Ibid., 182-185.

34. Ibid., 55.

35. Ibid., 55-56.

36. Perry, *Malcolm*, 160-166.

IN CONCLUSION: WHERE DO WE GO FROM HERE?

ELIZABETH A. PETERSON

It is sometimes difficult to understand why there has been a continual struggle among African Americans to realize equity in educational opportunity and in turn to realize social and economic equality as a race. Although there have been many advancements, we find as we enter a new century that a large number of black Americans find themselves in oppressive conditions similar to those of their slave ancestors.

The individuals highlighted in this text made a significant contribution to their people, yet their personalities, motives, and outcomes were very different. Each of them in many regards "swam against the tide" and were rejected by or rejected others who were in reality trying to accomplish the same thing. In the end the individuals themselves do not seem as important as the goals they were trying to reach.

Charlotte Forten found that she did not have the stamina to teach people who, in her mind, were primitive and simplistic. She was an elitist, though well meaning. With her classical upbringing she found it difficult to understand people whose background was so different from her own. As a black woman she had felt the sting of racism, but could not help condescending to those that many would consider her own people. Did she help those that she served? Most assuredly. That she was even willing to leave her comfortable surroundings to serve and teach is a testimony to her deep commitment and courage. But it is also to her credit that she finally left teaching and returned to her native Philadelphia to continue the fight against racism in a different manner.

Mary Ann Cary recognized that educational advancement and hard work were the key to the uplift of African American people and that prejudice and bigotry could only be eliminated through better understanding between the races. She believed that integrating schools was the means to bringing the races together, not for the purpose of making black people more like whites, or for racial assimilation, but for increased awareness and understanding. She became disillusioned, however, when she found that her view came under attack not only by whites that wished to preserve segregation, but by other blacks who chose to attack her rather than support her cause. It was difficult for her to acknowledge that she could not even depend upon her own people, those that she was trying so hard to help, to support her. She was forced to concede that racism was perhaps too strong and deeply imbedded for her to fight alone. Nearly one hundred years would pass from the time when Cary established her school for the dream of school integration to be realized.

This lack of support and cooperation is most evident in the case of Washington and Du Bois. But the fallout from their bitter feud touched others as well. The issues that drove a wedge between Washington and Du Bois finally closed The Institute for Colored Youth in Philadelphia. Fanny Jackson Coppin saw both moral and financial support for her efforts dwindle away as Booker T. Washington was increasingly recognized as the spokesman for black people. Although she was a successful teacher and mentor to many young adults, she could not continue her work when support from the recognized leadership was not forthcoming.

Marcus Garvey with the UNIA initiated perhaps the most ambitious program of all. Yet, today many African Americans have no idea of the tremendous role Garvey played. Though he touched many lives, Garvey was and still is considered by many to be out of the mainstream and therefore his leadership is suspect. What is most dismaying is that this perception is held probably by as many African Americans as whites.

When all is considered, perhaps, Alain Locke faired better than other black leaders of his time in that his brilliance and integrity as an individual won him respect from other black leaders as well as acceptance from wealthy benefactors who had an interest in the affairs of the "Negro."

In his position he helped other aspiring black men and women find an audience for their works. But more importantly he was able to bring interested scholars together to work on a common agenda.

His role as an early leader in the AAAE in bringing forth the African American agenda is noteworthy.

The needs of the black community have been and continue to be complex. At the same time there has been a tendency by both African American leaders and white benefactors to look for a single solution and a single leader to bring forth a solution to these very complex issues. What kind of educational program is needed for the African American community? Many different kinds programs are needed to build a viable productive African American community. Perhaps it is time for African American educators to put aside philosophical differences and work together, recognizing that the community as a whole can only benefit from cooperation.

It is because of this kind of cooperation that Septima Clark was able to elicit such a positive response in the black community. The urgency of the Civil Rights Movement spurred interest from all levels in the Freedom Schools. Supporters rallied to guarantee success and detractors became just another foe to be defeated as part of the greater program. Yet, even with the noted success of such a broad-based grassroots effort, the program lost its effectiveness after the death of Dr. King as the Civil Rights Movement in general moved in a different direction. It is difficult to sustain a program that draws its strength and appeal from the charisma of one individual.

Malcolm X's work continues to resonate in the black community long after his death as it did in his lifetime. Although Malcolm X had many detractors, his message came at a time when social and political unrest was at its highest and when those who were most disenfranchised were ready to listen. Malcolm X's teachings were rooted in his strong sense of history. As more and more people were attracted to the teachings of Elijah Muhammad and the Nation of Islam, he used his gift of ministry to teach black people to claim their history, and understand that they were not inferior, and to encourage them to empower themselves to defeat a toxic and racist social order.

After the fires of the sixties died down, it was necessary to heal and rebuild. During the next decade black leaders directed their attention to monitoring the implementation of the newly signed Civil Rights Act. As part of that legislation public schools were to be desegregated. No longer would it me legal for public schools to remain racially segregated. Finally, Mary Ann Shadd's dream had come true. Students and faculty had to be dispersed in such a way that ratios were upheld. It seemed at the time that this was the thing to do. If done correctly all African American children would have equal access to all of the educational privileges that they had long been denied, and they would graduate from high school as young adults who were as prepared as any other to meet the challenges of an increasingly technological society. These young adults would be prepared to move into good jobs that could support them and their families, or they would continue their schooling. It was thought that young African American men and women would have better and equal access to colleges and universities, vocational and technical schools, and skilled apprenticeship programs. This was the freedom that many hoped would come out of the intense struggle of the sixties.

Where are we today at the beginning of the twenty-first century? It is true that more African Americans today have moved into the middle class. It is true that African Americans overall have increased their wealth and that you can find black representation in almost all fields and professions. In the past ten years blacks have been elected to and appointed to key government positions. But at the same time the gap between those blacks who have made it and those who have not has widened. More black women and children live in poverty than ever before, and black men are more likely to be incarcerated than any other group.

In the 1970's policies such as Affirmative Action were enforced, scholarships and grants were set aside for minorities and women. This enabled more African American youths than ever before to go to school. Due to federally mandated desegregation, large state-supported schools opened their doors to black students and private, Ivy League schools actively recruited black students. At the close of the twentieth century policies like Affirmative Action have come under fire. Some states such as Texas and California voted to eliminate Affirmative Action all together. What does all of this mean? It means that many blacks and other minorities are finding that it is more difficult for them to gain access to good schools and employment. Grades and test scores serve as gate-keeping measures that keep many poor and minority youths out. University officials and employers will say that these measures are fair and unbiased despite research that clearly indicates that standardized tests favor the middle class. They also do not acknowledge the fact that social networks and connections still count for most academic admissions and hiring. The "good old boy" system is still at work.

Therefore there are many African Americans who would maintain that they are no better off today. They contend that the environment in this nation is still unfavorable to African Americans. Racial prejudice is still very much a factor that affects the lives of every American. It sometimes seems that we've hit a brick wall and that no one even wants to talk about the issue or as one woman remarked, "I thought we took care of all that in the sixties."

Why hasn't another major educational initiative grown out of the black community to address some of the growing unfavorable trends? Has the commitment to education died? Not really, but there is disillusionment. As stated before, many African Americans believed that with the signing of the Civil Rights Act they would have complete access to a quality education and later to job training and employment. Unfortunately desegregation is not synonymous with integration. Schools, neighborhoods, and the workforce was desegregated, not integrated. Prejudices that have long separated the races have not been fully resolved. In many communities as the public schools opened their doors to blacks, the whites fled or opted for private schools. In many urban areas "white flight" drastically lowed the tax base which supports the public schools. As more blacks entered the middle class they too abandoned the cities and the traditionally black neighborhoods in order to offer their children the better educational opportunities that were available in suburban and private schools. As a result many African American children have been and still are recipients of a below standard education. As they grow into adulthood they lack the basic skills that they need to leave their environment. They find that they are trapped in a continuous cycle of poverty. The disillusionment comes from feeling that there is no way out—school does not seem to be the answer in these communities where so few seem to benefit from them.

Some groups still continue their efforts to provide educational activities in the black community. The efforts of the Nation of Islam in particular should be commended. Rather than suspend their efforts, the Nation of Islam has continued to reach out to disenfranchised blacks, especially black males. Their message of black pride and empowerment has turned around many young men who would otherwise have turned to drugs and crime. While some may take exception to Muslim practices and teachings, they still must be given credit for the positive influence they have had on some.

It is not too late to recapture the dream. The twenty-first century offers new hope. There are black leaders at all levels and in all occupations who are models of who we want to be. It is as important today as it has been in the past to have quality adult education programs in the African American community. In the past the debate was based on a belief held by many that one type of educational program could be designed as a "fix it" for the black community. The opposing positions of Booker T. Washington and W.E.B. Du Bois represent the passion of this debate. Perhaps it does not really matter so much whether a liberal arts education or a vocational education is the focus for African Americans. Perhaps the focus needs to be more concentrated on the positive message that an education of any kind that prepares one to meet the challenges of today is valuable. What kind of education should be determined by the varying needs, interests, and aspirations of each individual. What should remain constant is the message that as black people and as Americans we've made a significant contribution to this nation and the world.

We must remember what we have learned from those who have brought us this far. We must retrace the steps of the leaders and teachers who have traveled before us. The hope and inspiration that dedicated black teachers like Fanny Coppin, Charlotte Forten Grimke, Mary Ann Cary, and Septima Clark gave to their students kept them going. The brilliance of black scholars such as Alain Locke and W. E. B. Du Bois encouraged others to utilize their talents and aspire to greatness. Booker T. Washington focused on self-help, hard work, and community pride. Marcus Garvey's and Malcolm X's message was an even stronger appeal for self reliance and empowerment and social action. These lessons from the past are just as important today. We must also learn from the mistakes of those who preceded us. We can no longer let personalities get in the way of good ideas. We must find ways to work together for the good of all. The ultimate goal–freedom–is more important than any one individual. We must remember the struggles of all the other black men and women, not just those named in this volume, who have given their lives in the pursuit of the promise of freedom. Those who have helped light the path on the FREEDOM ROAD.

INDEX